HOW TO GET INTO YOUR DREAM UNIVERSITY

THE DEFINITIVE GUIDE FOR IB STUDENTS

HOW TO GET INTO YOUR DREAM UNIVERSITY

THE DEFINITIVE GUIDE FOR IB STUDENTS

ALEXANDER ZOUEV
ROMAN ZOUEV
ZOUEV PUBLISHING

Published 2021

ISBN 978-1-9163451-4-0, paperback.

This book is dedicated to the university counselors, IB coordinators and IB teachers who go the extra mile for their students.

Table of Contents

HOW TO GET INTO YOUR DREAM UNIVERSITY

CHAPTER 1

INTRODUCTION

Congratulations on obtaining the **only** university guidebook aimed specifically at helping students enrolled in the International Baccalaureate Diploma Program get into the university of their dreams. By picking up and reading this book you are already well on your way to making sure your journey to higher education is a smooth and successful process.

I still vividly remember filling out my own applications for UK universities way back in 2007. I was lucky enough to have the guidance of my older brother (and co-author), but also two well-experienced university coordinators (one specializing in UK university applications, the other in US colleges) and a handful of super supportive teachers who themselves studied at top-tier universities around the world.

A lot has changed in the last fifteen years. As an EU student, I remember that my university fees were around £2,000 per year (it is now around £9,000[1] - thank you Brexit!) and we had a choice of six universities (it is now down to five). The UCAS online system was still in its infancy, and my application to Oxford was done by hand (which was super stressful for me as I was worried that they would judge my awful handwriting!) Acceptance and rejection letters arrived not by email, but by post into your mailbox.

Even though much has changed, the rules and strategies of applying to top universities are largely the same. One thing that certainly has not changed is just how important it is to get your application right. You are submitting something that will decide the next 3-4 years of your life.

Thinking about university is also something that you cannot postpone too far into your IB journey. In fact, even whilst choosing your IB subjects in pre-IB, you should already be thinking about how this will impact or limit your choices (more on this later).

Before we get into the specifics however, I would like to outline my motivation for putting this book together and why it is important for you to read it. First and foremost, it is no secret that the International Baccalaureate program is still not where it should be in terms of worldwide recognition and university acceptance. While the program has made leaps and bounds over the last few decades, there is still a long way to go before it can overtake the A-Levels or AP in terms of popularity and acknowledgment. The implications of this for current students are immense. Almost all the information and help (both free and paid) is not really written with the IB student in mind. This book hopes to change that.

At the outset, the IB program's relative obscurity may not seem like much of a worry. After all, most of the information on university websites is helpful regardless of where you studied or which high school program you are taking. However, when you start to

[1] In fairness, UK home students also pay much higher fees these days – but at least they can get interest-free loans

consider the fact that IB students tend to come from foreign places, unfamiliar with local education system and requirements, you start to feel that there is a gap in information and extra help is needed.

I am also often approached by students who say that, even though, they had predictions of 42 and 7, 6, 6 in HL, they failed to get an offer from LSE/Oxbridge/Harvard/Yale/etc. I tell them that I have known more than a handful of students with grade 45 predictions (and final result!) who also did not get those offers. It happens. But the inevitable follow-up question is: 'Why? What do I need to do to get an offer?'

This book aims to shed some light on that question and many others. We have split this guide into some introductory chapters and then some regional chapters (the UK, the USA, the Netherlands, Canada, Australia, Germany, and Hong Kong) and each chapter will guide you through the application process and what you can do as an IB student to maximize your chances of getting into the best universities.

Choosing which university to attend, or whether to go to university at all after two intense years of the International Baccalaureate program is no easy decision. This guidebook aims to help those students who have their hearts set on higher education at the university of their dreams. But first, let's answer some basic questions...

How to use this book?

Writing a university guide for IB students proved to be a more monumental task than we expected. The main difficulty lay in the fact that application processes vary considerably across countries and continents, so we did not want UK applicants to waste their time reading about SAT exams, and likewise we don't want to confuse those applying to US colleges with all this talk about UCAS.

Here is how we suggest you read this book:

1. Read the first five chapters which deal with general advice and contain information that *every* IB student should know.
2. We then suggest you also read our UK chapter as it will cover the references and also offer some tips of how to choose a course.
3. Thereafter, flip to the relevant chapter that concerns your potential country destination.

What countries recognize the IB?

IB Diploma students apply to institutions in more than 100 countries each year. Many universities are now aware of the IB Diploma and its benefits, thanks to the IBO's continued efforts to assure its global acceptance. The Diploma, however, is still interpreted differently in different countries. As IB students apply to universities in particular regions more frequently than in others, overall awareness is not necessarily uniform. In IB-specific admissions policies, several universities explicitly specify what they anticipate of IB applicants. Some of them will be discussed in more detail in later chapters.

Do universities like the IB?

They certainly do! Most colleges do not express an official preference for one qualification over another, and each application is judged on its own merits. However, studies of IBDP students in the United States, the United Kingdom, Australia, Mexico, and China reveal that IBDP students are more likely to continue undergraduate studies. They are also more likely to gain admission to prestigious and competitive universities than their non-IB peers. The esteemed 'Ivy League' colleges in the US, for instance, are between 3% and 13% more likely to accept IB students than other applicants who did not do the IB. Better still, once they are at university, IB students are more likely to continue to excel academically than their classmates!

Do I need any other qualifications to apply?

In most cases, you'll be able to apply to universities based only on your IB exam results. There are, however, certain exceptions. Some competitive US universities like Harvard and Yale require you to sit the multiple-choice SAT Reasoning Test, along with 2-3 SAT Subject Tests. You could choose to sit these in your Higher-Level subjects, if you feel that these are your strongest.

Certain UK universities in oversubscribed courses will require applicants to sit admissions tests. For instance, many law applicants must take the LNAT (Law National Aptitude Test) before applying. Similarly, most aspiring medics will have to take either the BMAT (Biomedical Admissions Test) or UKCAT (UK Clinical Aptitude Test). Some competitive universities such as Oxford and Cambridge even have their own admissions tests for certain subjects. Make sure that you find out exactly what will be expected of you in good time and prepare early.

Pro Tip: if you need to take external tests like BMAT or UKCAT, find out early on where in your city you can take them and when. Start studying for them early, but don't let it take over your life!

Will my subject choices affect where I can apply?

For certain courses, yes. As ever, each university has its own policy, so, do your research. Universities often will require you to achieve a certain grade in specific subjects at HL or SL. As a general rule, courses in the natural sciences, medicine and engineering will have stricter subject requirements than arts and humanities. For example, the Chemistry course at Oxford University requires 40 points overall (including core), with a 7 in Chemistry HL and a 6/7 in Mathematics HL, or a 7 in Mathematics SL plus a second science with 7 HL (...ouch!). Equally, different university systems have different requirements (for example, German universities are quite particular). Always check the website of the university you are considering applying to as early as possible to ensure that you are not limiting your options.

We hope that this book will spur a wider movement where universities and independent educational guides take greater notice of IB students and recognize that the rise in the popularity of the program is very real. We also hope that this information is digested properly by IB students, so that we can have even more feedback and university guides in future editions.

CHAPTER 2

HOW TO SET YOUR APPLICATION APART

This chapter provides some introductory general tips on how you can set yourself apart from other candidates when applying to university in any part of the world. An IB qualification means that a student is undoubtably at an advantage. However, competition is still rife, and top IB scores alone aren't enough to secure a place at university. These tips could help students set themselves apart from the thousands of other university applications and stand out from the crowd.

1. The right extracurricular activity counts

Consider the situation from the perspective of a university's admissions team, who have to filter through thousands of applications trying to find the right candidates. Virtually, all of the students applying will have achieved top grades and will include an array of interesting extracurricular activities in their applications.

Being able to demonstrate something unique in an extracurricular experience will help an application move to the top of the pile. This is particularly true if the activity is closely linked to the subject a student has chosen to study or aligns with an issue close to their heart.

For example, one IB student that I tutored last year had a love of literature and writing. He set up a program where high school volunteers worked with critically ill children to help them create their own storybook.

This non-profit initiative helped children write, illustrate, and have full creative control over their very own storybook. After their creation, the stories were published and delivered with a fluffy toy animal and certification of completion to the children. The scheme created a welcome distraction for the children and impressed the admissions office of the University of Chicago, and they offered the student a place at their university.

Basically, you should be looking to do some activities that make the university look good *for having you as one of their students!* Do something that both you and they can be proud of.

2. Expanding learning beyond academic study

It is hugely beneficial for IB students to take their passion for their specialist field to the next level, by engaging in activities that have a positive impact on their local community and beyond. This also demonstrates key skills such as leadership, problem solving and creativity.

The fourth revolution has begun, heralding a time of steep technological innovation and advancement. Candidates who can show leadership in identifying a problem and finding a novel way to solve it will stand out from the crowd. These skills are highly valued both by universities and employers.

For example, another recent IB graduate that I worked with has recycled over 5,000lbs of electronic waste with the help of other passionate advocates, after noticing the huge amount of waste having devastating effects on environment.

His organization acts as a middleman between consumers of technologies and government-licensed recyclers. Students collect unused and discarded electronics (e-waste), and recyclers separate and extract metals which are then melted down.

Another girl I mentored last year helped children receive much needed prosthetic arms. She worked with a company that makes prostheses that are personalized to meet the needs of individuals and changed the lives of many children. These are all great examples of how students have used their creativity and skills to find solutions to some of the most pressing global issues.

3. Be authentic

When students are choosing extracurricular activities, it's key to choose a topic, issue or activity that truly represents the student. The right activities enable a student to grow and develop, as well as show the university admissions officers who they really are and what they have to offer.

Admissions officers have been doing their jobs for many years (in some instances, decades) so they know exactly how to sniff out the BS and can detect fakeness from a mile away. It is best to actually be a well-rounded and passionate student - instead of trying to merely give the impression of being one.

The crucial advice for DP students: applying your knowledge in purposeful activities that are important to you will stretch your understanding and skillset, and that is something that many universities will value. This could be the thing that puts you one step ahead of the competition.

Finally, there is also another way in which the IB will set you apart - once you are already at the university of your dreams. By taking the IB, many aspects of your new course will become relatively easy. If you talk to alumni about the benefits of the IB, most will mention that after doing it, college becomes much easier as you are used to the workload.

University students often tend to find the workload in college suffocating. IB will definitely help you with that. There are also numerous other advantages. IB will help you become a better researcher, become more independent in studies (which is a huge factor in college). There is probably no other curriculum that better prepares you for university, and for this reason you are already at an advantage!

IB - strenuous, difficult, rewarding and respectable

IB - better researcher

IB - helps you to become more independent in your studies

IB - College / University becomes much easier.

IB - EE - gave you a sense of how much writing is involved in College

IB - CAS - involved in the community

IB - TOK

IB - learn a new language

IB - Culture appreciation

CHAPTER 3

THE PERSONAL STATEMENT

[This chapter was written with primarily the UK/UCAS personal statement in mind - however, the advice here is also largely applicable for applying anywhere in the world. We have included region-specific tips in each of the relevant country chapters. We do suggest reading through this chapter in its entirety, even if you are not applying to the UK]

Put yourself into the shoes of a university admissions officer. You must go through thousands of personal statements, the vast majority of which come from A-level students in both private, but mainly public schools in the UK. They will write about how they nearly became head boy/girl and how they really enjoyed their participation in the Duke of Edinburgh award (if neither of these things made sense to you, don't worry - they are terms that only a typical British student would normally understand). The point I am trying to make is that the vast majority of students applying through the British school system have very little that will differentiate themselves amongst the other candidates. They will talk about their GCSE's and how they are coping with their A-Levels and how they play football for their local team. All of this is fine, but it gets boring and repetitive. Admissions officers are looking for something with added spice.

Here is where the IB Diploma program comes into play. You need to use the fact that the IB program is not as well-known as the A-levels to your advantage. Write about how your Extended Essay gave you a good sense of what a university level paper requires. Explain how CAS enabled you to participate in the community and make a difference. Talk about TOK, and lab reports, and learning a foreign language. Those of you studying in International Schools, make sure to play the 'culture card'. Admission officers eat that stuff up. Talk about how you have friends from all over the world, and how you have learnt about new cultures and religions, and this has made you see the world in a different light. Do you catch my drift?

You need to realize that your application is unique in the sense that you are studying in an environment that is vastly different from most other applicants. The IB Diploma program is difficult and strenuous, but also highly respectable and rewarding. You need to convey these messages across your personal statement, and then add something extra to make yourself stand out from other IB applicants.

Therefore, the personal statement is perhaps the trickiest (and arguably most important) part of the application process. It can also easily turn into a 'catch-22' situation. Everyone you consult will have their own opinion and you are bombarded with advice, sometimes contradictory. The universities themselves sometimes contribute to the confusion by giving misleading advice.[2]

The vast majority of admission offices and tutors claim that the personal statement is of utmost importance, and this is clearly true for courses that are oversubscribed, and which receive hundreds of more high-quality applications than available places (as well as, obviously, Oxbridge applications). In such cases, the personal statement is your only real opportunity to distinguish yourself from other, equally qualified, candidates. It may be useful here to make a distinction between the Russell Group universities and the rest.[3] The Russell Group are the most competitive and, some would say, elitist of UK universities. Therefore, their admission policies are typically different from other universities. They are also frequently accused of favoring independent schools over state schools.[4] Even as of 2021, this is still very much the case.

Pro Tip: The majority of IB applicants will be in a separate category. Even if there is a private school bias, this will not disadvantage the average IB applicant – so you should not worry!

We are not interested in investigating the possible bias against state schools but instead seeing how we can use this information to our benefit with regards to the personal statement. It is evident that the personal statement plays a much more important role in the admissions process for Russel Group universities, but even here the role is rather ambiguous.

However, this information is not true for the vast majority of courses, many of which are undersubscribed. These are typically

---

[2] One university prospectus included advice that it is important, in the personal statement, to indicate a clear interest and commitment to that university. This is misleading advice since the same personal statement is read by all applicant choices!

[3] The Russell Group is a self-selected association of twenty-four universities in the United Kingdom. Its members are sometimes perceived as being the most prestigious universities in the country. See https://en.wikipedia.org/wiki/Russell_Group for more information.

[4] This is slowly changing, but has a long way to go: https://www.theguardian.com/education/2020/oct/10/britains-best-universities-are-dominated-by-private-schools-could-i-help-level-the-playing-field

the courses that appear as 'extra'.[5] They accept applicants after the January 15th closing date and usually list, in 'clearing', available courses with places to fill.

For these courses, the personal statement does not count as much and is only really used to decide borderline cases. If an applicant has the actual or predicted grades, an offer will usually be given, and it is quite possible that the personal statement will not be read at all. One admissions officer confided in me that she only read the applicant who did not present a wholly convincing academic profile. Her opinion was that there is very little 'original truth' in these statements - and the vast majority are utterly predictable. What the university wants to see is evidence of academic ability, which will enable the applicant to complete the course successfully.

A strong personal statement and a predicted IB score of 38 may secure an *offer* for a place on a competitive course, but it is the actual score of 38 that will secure the *place*. It is academic achievement that the universities are most interested in. This is reflected very clearly by the 'adjustment' process which has been recently introduced - which allows candidates who do better than expected to request consideration for courses that have a higher entry requirement than their firm choice (more on this later).

Pro Tip: try not to go into too much detail about CAS or extracurriculars that are irrelevant to your course (simply because you are limited in your word count!). For example, don't waste time on explaining how you play in a band if you are applying for a Math degree.

The aim of this chapter is to provide a realistic appraisal of the role of the personal statement and to offer practical guidelines on how to go about producing a convincing and appropriate statement (including what to avoid and how to be original). Our hope is that

---

[5] An extra listing means that the course is open for applications and is available for applicants who have been unsuccessful with all their applications.

we will be able to dispel some of the many myths which surround this topic and to provide you with some concrete tips that you, as an IB student, can use in constructing your personal statement. Our opinions will be supported by evidence from actual admissions officers and also the findings of two important studies: the Pearson Think Tank and the Sutton Trust.

Busting PS Myths

The first myth we need to dispel regarding the personal statement is that it is necessary for the statement to be completely *personal*, in the sense that it is *exclusively* the product of the applicant.

Pro Tip: No professional university counsellor would allow an applicant to send off their original personal statement without at least some minor suggestions and corrections!

Most private schools have entire teams of dedicated advisors who provide support and guidance for the writing of the personal statement. Consequently, the result frequently bears very little resemblance to the applicant's first draft. Left to themselves, applicants would tend to produce very poorly written descriptive accounts of their achievements and rely on cliches and exaggerations.

The drafting and rewriting of the personal statement are, therefore, necessary for the majority of those applicants to the most competitive courses. Unfortunately, this raises the bar for all other applicants. As long as nothing has been copied directly from some written source, it is impossible for the UCAS or the university to know if the personal statement is the applicant's own work. This puts the applicant who wants to 'go at it alone' at a serious disadvantage and makes the writing of a truly original and interesting personal statement almost impossible.

A university may suspect that a personal statement is too sophisticated to be the work of the applicant but fail to detect any evidence of actual plagiarism. In this case, they must give the applicant the benefit of the doubt. Experienced counsellors and advisors are good at writing convincing personal statements for prospective applicants and competitive universities are used to reading statements that have been heavily 'processed'. In fact, some admissions tutors would be offended if an applicant did not take the personal statement seriously enough to seek outside advice and help. The danger is that the personal statement ceases to be a useful criterion for admissions and will be increasingly ignored by some universities.

Pro Tip: remember that the Personal Statement is **NOT** like the common application (US) essay - do not make it some elaborate story. This is important for students to understand who are applying to both UK and US institutions.

The Pearson Think Tank has some very interesting information in the form of quotes from actual Russell Group University admissions officers that shed some light on how they view the personal statement.[6] We have reproduced some of these quotes here:

1. "The use and importance of personal statements was highly variable both between and within institutions. In some universities, and for some less competitive courses, they were not used at all in assessment of the application, whilst in others these were important in differentiating between applicants and gaining a sense of their suitability for the course.

[6] For more information see Candy, S. (*Un)informed Choices? University admissions* practices and social mobility. London: Pearson, 2013.

2. “Sometimes it makes no difference; sometimes it makes all the difference.”

3. “I don’t see it would make any difference if they weren’t there frankly, because those who are told what to write and all the rest of it ... and not all of them are true.”

4. “I don’t like personal statements, there is too much evidence, anecdotal evidence about the role of teachers in personal statements and there has to be a concern that the better, the more privileged the school, the more help is on hand to creating personal statements, that’s why we down-weight them. We distrust them.”

5. “We do assume that the applicant has written it themselves and that it is something valid to look at.”

6. “I’ve spoken to Heads of private schools about the question of how much help they give students in writing statements, they said, ‘well they’re paying £7,000 a term of course we give them a lot of help, that’s what they’re paying for’.”

7. “We have so many overqualified applicants if we just went on grades we’d accept everybody, so we must use the personal statement ... it tells me something about the applicant, it tells me something about the way they view the subject and the kind of work they want to do, and that is important for a subject like politics which can be taught in a number of different ways.”

The above selection of quotes gives some indication of the diversity of opinion regarding the personal statement. It would appear that academic admissions tutors attach more importance to it than do general admissions staff. The research by Dr. Steven Jones of

Manchester University for the Sutton Trust confirms the ambiguity of the personal statement, and although its perspective is more interested in the disadvantage to state schools, it also provides evidence of inconsistency in its use as an admissions criterion. He goes on to recommend that "Personal statements should be more than an excuse to highlight past advantages. Applicants should outline how they might contribute to campus life, and universities should make it clear that applicants are not penalized for lacking opportunities in the past due to family circumstances."[7]

Universities claim that they are looking for a truthful statement from applicants, but I have my doubts whether a statement that is so obviously written by a confused applicant, with no outside help, would, in fact, be seriously considered. Who would risk beginning their statement with the following introduction?

"I am really confused about what I need to write in this statement and how I can make myself seem interesting and committed to my chosen course. I think that I would enjoy studying XYZ but as I have never studied this subject before, I honestly cannot be certain. I could pretend that I have read numerous books on the subject, like everybody else does, but this would not be true. I personally do not think that the cost of £9000 a year is worth it, but my parents insist that I need a university education. I am quite a good student and think that I would be able to get through this course and get a degree at the end.

Like the majority of students, I will not get involved in university life and do not want to play sports or participate in plays and do not feel the need to lie about this. I realize that I am not presenting myself as an especially desirable candidate, but I am essentially no different from the majority of applicants except that I am telling the truth."

---

[7] See Sutton Trust, *Research*, suttontrust.com (2014)

Such a statement has the merit of being honest, but it would be described as naïve and inappropriate, and few university counsellors would allow it to be sent.

Personally, I feel that some admissions tutors would find the honesty of such a statement perhaps refreshing and would welcome the fact that, at least, it has been written by the applicant and not a professional advisor. Nonetheless, conventional wisdom dictates that the raw truth needs to be tempered and that qualities and attributes need to be presented in a modest and favorable manner.

The second myth about personal statements you will often hear is that you absolutely must 'tell the truth'. The example above is an example of how telling the truth is not necessarily a good thing. That is not to say that you should lie, but you should not feel obliged to include so-called 'incriminating truths'. In other words, your real reasons for wanting to go to university do not necessarily have to be honestly stated.

Pro Tip: You are expected to be positive about your desire to study a particular course and to express some knowledge about the course and its content.

Nonetheless, my experience talking to admission tutors has indicated that they do appreciate the occasional honesty.

For example, if you say you want to study business because you will be taking over the family business. This is not entirely inappropriate and shows some long-term aspiration consistent with the course. In contrast, to say you want to study Law because lawyers can earn a large salary is probably not the best way to express interest in your course.

What to Avoid

Now that we have discussed some general points regarding the personal statement, we can move on to look at the 'Do's and Don'ts.

Pro Tip: Avoid cliches at all costs! They induce nausea and your admissions counsellors will roll their eyes and chuck your application to the back of the pile.

The worst offender here is the cursed phrase 'ever since I was a young child' - which claims an interest since literal childhood. Nobody is gullible enough to believe that you wanted to be a philosopher since age 3, or that being in a car accident as an infant inspired you to study medicine and become a doctor. It is best to present your passions in a more believable and acceptable way. You should present your interest in the subject by somehow linking it to your current IB subjects, or by linking it to important current events and developments.

Pro Tip: Use your IB subjects here to your advantage. E.g., if you want to study business, talk about how something you are currently studying in IB business and management has really inspired you.

Prospective Law students should not link their interest to a popular TV series or film, even if it happens to be true. It is much better to link the interest with some current event or legal issue that is controversial, such as the rights of minorities, or the importance of the rule of law. This type of link also has the advantage of showing your knowledge and interest in current issues.

For those who are truly inspired by a particular course, it is essential to convey this interest in a believable way. The best way to do this is to discuss a current issue or development which will show that you take a knowledgeable interest in the subject and that you are familiar with such topics. Avoid making grandiose claims about books that you have read and their impact on you. Concentrate, instead, on new developments and the impact that you anticipate from these.

If your interest is Economics, it is better to present your view on a current issue, such as unemployment in Europe or income inequality, than to claim that you have been inspired after reading the works of Keynes. Similarly, a History applicant should try to present an interest in a new development or interpretation that is controversial. This applies to all subjects, and it is only possible to claim genuine interest if some knowledge of recent developments is shown.

Pro Tip: You cannot be convincingly interested in a subject if you do not know what current issues are being discussed!

If you do not know what these recent developments are, you should find out by reading journals or articles online. It is always better to display this knowledge meaningfully than to claim having read a book.

To say 'I am interested in politics and economics and read the Economist every week' might be true but it tells the admissions tutor nothing of value and cannot be verified. It is much better to make a reference to a specific issue that you have read about and indicate an interest in exploring this topic in greater depth at university.

If you are an EU or overseas applicant, you could refer to some event in your country that links up with the subject that you want to study. Similarly, if you have lived in different countries, you should show how this has given you a better understanding of cultural differences and an insight into alternative beliefs and attitudes.

Pro Tip: Use your IB 'learner profile' and international experience (if you are studying outside of the UK) to your advantage! Talk about local cultural issues and how this has been integrated into your IB Diploma. Admissions officers love that stuff!

Universities welcome diversity and will want their courses to have a good mix of different cultures and backgrounds. Speaking several languages and having lived in many countries makes you potentially interesting and these points need to be stated to show that they have contributed to your open-minded outlook. The fact that all IB applicants have at least one language, in addition to English, is a definite advantage and needs to be pointed out.

You should not present lists of achievements or interests because it sounds like showing off and provides very little useful information. The fact that you have volunteered to visit old people every Christmas since age 13 is very admirable, but it is much more useful to say how this has affected your personality and development (as you are used to expressing this in your CAS reflections).

Pro Tip: you can BS some things to demonstrate more interest... For example, I wrote about readings academic journal articles in my free time, which I don't actually do (but I would be prepared to lie about this if asked in an interview!).

As a general rule, you should always mention an achievement or interest by saying how it affected you and specifically, how it has made you a better student or person. Many IB students participate in MUN[8] and other international debating tournaments. To simply state this is not enough. You need to show how the experience has had an impact on you. For example, having to argue a case that you do not agree with forces you to be objective. It may also enhance your diplomatic skills and your ability to speak in public. It is these skills that are important to mention rather than the event itself.

Similarly, with volunteer work it is important to say what you have gained from it rather than just mentioning it. All IB applicants must perform some community service as part of their CAS program and this is potentially a useful point to include, but rather than simply

[8] MUN = Model United Nations. See https://www.nmun.org/

stating it, you should elaborate on how this has affected you and made you a more accomplished individual. The ability to express your contribution modestly and with humility is very important, so you must never simply brag and boast your achievements.

Pro Tip: make sure to talk about your EE and CAS in your personal statement!

IB students have two further advantages which should be mentioned in their personal statement. The first is the Extended Essay; this will hopefully be in the subject area of your chosen university course. Your aim will be to show how you enjoyed the challenge of researching your topic and how this prepares you for the skills needed at university. It is also an opportunity for you to emphasize your interest in a chosen subject area. If your Extended Essay is not in your chosen course area of interest, it can still be usefully referred to as an opportunity for studying a topic in depth, which constituted a challenge, by being in an area outside of your comfort zone. Even though the truth is that you chose to do your EE in History because it is much easier than finding a suitable topic in Physics, it is better to try and provide a more positive (but believable!) reason for this choice.

You can also try to find a clever way to link the two. For example, my EE was in Mathematics (even thought I was applying for Economics courses at university), but I still managed to write a couple of lines about how understanding the complex equations was an important skill that was required for studying economics at an undergraduate level.

The second advantage for the IB applicant is the TOK course. This should prepare them for critical thinking and questioning of knowledge which are both skills that the universities value. The specific essay title that the candidate selects can be used as an example of a particular insight relevant to their chosen course of study.

Pro Tip: Overall, the key is not just to *tell* the admissions officer why you are keen and capable of studying this course, but to *show* them. Use evidence to back up what you are saying at every opportunity.

How to Structure the Personal Statement

The UCAS personal statement has a maximum length of **4000 characters,** which roughly translates to **600 words**. You should not feel obliged to fill the whole space, but if applying to a highly competitive course, you would probably to use up everything.

Here is some advice on how you can better structure your personal statement:

1. You need to begin with a short introductory paragraph that attempts to capture the interest of the admissions tutor so that he/she wants to read on.

Pro Tip: do not mention facts here that appear elsewhere in the application (e.g., my name is Mark, and I am applying for courses is Psychology - this information is already known, and you need to save words!

Depending on how much of a risk taker you are, you can start with some humor. However, most counsellors will not let you take such a risk. A few years ago, an applicant for drama stated in her personal statement that she realized that as a dyslexic actor she would probably end up working in a bra. Whether the admissions tutors were amused or not is unknown, but she got offers from all of her choices.

A safer, and thus better, option is to begin by describing the impact that a recent event had on you and your desire to study a particular subject. The opening should be used to establish your credentials and justify your interest in your chosen subject.

2. You should then go on to link this interest to the academic subjects that you are studying and try to make some knowledgeable references to aspects of the degree course that you are especially interested in studying. Before making your choices, you should have gathered a lot of information about the courses that you are applying to, and you should use some of this information to show your awareness of what the courses offer. A cleverly worded reference can also convey your first preference to a particular university.

Your aim is to show an enthusiastic interest in your chosen subject, and this can be complemented by discussing any relevant work experience that you have undertaken. Again, the emphasis here should be on how this experience has inspired you and deepened your desire to pursue a particular subject.

Many courses have a subject requirement such as HL Mathematics for most Economics courses. When this is the case, it is very important to express both your ability and interest in Mathematics and the type of topics that you are enthusiastic about. To do this, you need to have carefully researched the course content of your choices.

Pro Tip: you will have multiple, multiple drafts for your personal statement and that's fine. I ended up having ELEVEN. Get everyone to read it - your teachers, your friends, your parents. Their help might turn out to be useless but there still might be some nuggets of gold there.

Here is one possible way you may structure your PS:

Introduction - state your purpose

Here you need to make it very clear what it is you want to study, and (briefly) why you want to study it. Originality is key. However, avoid being cliché. Just remember, what you do want to do is grab the Admissions Officer's attention. Often, the opening sentence is the hardest one to write.[9]

Pro Tip: I actually think that you **must** read a few sample personal statements before even starting to write your own - see the next section for eight examples.

Main Section - how have you come to the decision to choose your course? What has prepared you to take it on?

Here I suggest you think about two things...

1. School Work

- How have your studies so far led you towards your course choice?
- Are any of your IB subjects particularly relevant to your course?
- Don't be afraid to be specific - talk about which topics/modules (ideally relevant ones) that you found especially interesting, and *why*.
- Give evidence of how you have gained the key skills to succeed on your course.

2. Outside of School

How have you gone out of your way to learn about your subject of choice *beyond* just school? Examples of this might include:

[9]**Check out:** https://www.which.co.uk/money/university-and-student-finance/getting-into-uni/how-to-write-a-personal-statement-a3bfp7h4yv7s

- Reading books/articles not on your school reading lists
- Watching documentaries/listening to podcasts
- Attending talks/events/lectures on your subject
- Seeking relevant work experience
- Visiting museums/exhibitions
- Talking to experts in the field/current students

Extra Curriculars

Use this next section to show that you are an interesting individual who is capable of successfully pursuing several interests at once. This demonstrates the ability to manage your time well and is a skill which all successful university students have! Discuss your most impressive pastimes: clubs, positions of responsibility, awards, charitable efforts - CAS is perfect for this.

Conclusion

Briefly restate why you want to study your course, and why you are a strong applicant. Be concise, and ensure this section makes an impact - it will be the final thing the Admissions Officer reads, so leave a lasting impression!

In terms of how much to write for each section, here's my suggestion:

- Introduction - 15%
- Main Section - 60%
- Extra Curriculars - 15%
- Conclusion - 10%

Given the unique nature of the Personal Statement, it's a good idea to produce a few drafts. Play around with different examples and the structure of your statement. And do remember that **every statement is different** - if you read an older student's Personal Statement, don't feel that yours has to be similar, or follow the same format. Definitely get someone to read through your statement before you submit your application. It's always useful to have another set of eyes check for spelling/grammar mistakes you might have missed. Or if your school/college has a University/UCAS Advisor, ask them for feedback on your draft.

Pro Tip: Be crisp and precise in your PS; showcase your interests and your passions and complement that with some information on extracurriculars you have done.

Real Examples of Successful Personal Statements

<u>Example 1:</u> (Applicant for Economics - A. Zouev; 2006)

Having attended Antwerp International School in Belgium for the past twelve years has given me a very diverse background, where cultural diversity and tolerance as well as multitude of opinions was encouraged.

The reputation that English universities have earned is certainly justified, and I believe an English university will give me the best traditional education around. The manner of teaching students and the professionalism of the academic staff involved in England is what appeals most to me.

Economics, as a course, was only introduced to me last year when I decided to choose it as one of my six IB diploma subjects. Economics in particular surprised me, as it answers many questions on topics one experiences every day but never seems to ask, such as how resources are allocated and what determines prices. So far, my favorite topic was about externalities and market failure, and I am greatly looking forward to learning about monetary and fiscal policies. Having talked to graduates with Economics degrees, I understand that the depth at which these and other topics are studied at university level is much greater, which is why I want to pursue an Economics degree at university level.

I also really enjoy Higher Level Mathematics. Within the course, statistics is what appeals most to me. I believe that a good knowledge of statistics will help me in analyzing data when reading academic papers. Currently I am finishing an Extended Essay in Mathematics in which I analyze a 2000-year-old geometric question known as "Alhazen's Problem". I genuinely took great pleasure in going through the whole process of writing an essay – doing the research, organizing it, and editing my work.

I have a strong passion for football and having played as central defender at Varsity level for the past three years, I am hoping to continue this sport at university. Along with football, I have competed in NECIS competitions for swimming, basketball and track and field, winning medals in each sport. Being part of a team allowed me to see just how important communication, teamwork, and time-management skills are.

As editor of the Yearbook in my school for three years running, I have gained exposure to the responsibilities of deadlines and working under pressure. It was challenging, but it gave me an opportunity to self-tutor myself to previously unknown photo and page editing software and to successfully work together and lead other members of the team. It is hard to describe, but seeing the finished product always reminds me why I do this elective.

Getting involved with community service has definitely been one of my highlights over the past several years. Working to renovate and construct shelters for refugees in a CAS- organized (Creativity, Action, and Service component of the IB program) building project has allowed me to give something back to the community and grow as a person. In the coming November, I will also be attending a trip to Morocco to work at a local orphanage and help paint a local school near the city of Agadir.

I am excited by the idea of experiencing new challenges at University, such as working and living independently, and I know that I have enough ambition to succeed. I have a great hunger for expanding on and perfecting my existing economics knowledge, and I firmly believe that I can achieve that at university.

Example 2: (2015: Applicant for Education)

Since embarking on the IB Diploma program, I have developed a much more inquisitive approach to learning, and this has deepened my interest in education and the learning process. Why do I now like some subjects that I previously hated and why am I better at some subjects than others are questions that truly fascinate me. In addition, I am interested in the importance of the pre-school years to the education process and the significance of the home environment on academic development and achievement. All of these issues revolve around the formative years of childhood development, and I am certain that this is the subject area that I want to study at University.

[Note how the candidate explains exactly why they are interested in Education and how their experiences have contributed to this. Also note that their explanation is sincere and not exaggerated.]

Children are the future and I want to be a positive influence on this future. I am confident that pursuing a degree in Education will enable me to achieve this goal and I believe that my background experience has prepared me for this academic pathway. At the age of fifteen I took the initiative to undertake voluntary work under the guidance of "Tandem", a non-profit organization motivated by the need for the improvement of quality of life of the children and adults with disabilities, the awareness of society concerning disability and social inclusion and the empowerment of vulnerable social groups. For two consecutive years I spent two hours a week working with under-privileged children and helping them in any way I could.

The challenging situations that arose reinforced my desire to learn as much as possible, since I was able to ascertain the importance of education to a child's subsequent development. Additionally, in order to complement my practical expertise, I did a three-week internship with a kindergarten, where I was responsible for assisting the permanent staff, in addition to supervising the children during the break and completing evaluation forms. This experience confirmed my belief that the early stages of children's lives play a catalytic role in their development.

[Note that the professional and voluntary experience is presented in such a way as to reinforce the applicant's interest in and suitability for the course.]

I believe that the IB program has been a good preparation for my undergraduate studies, and it has helped me to overcome some of my academic weaknesses. Due to the numerous deadlines, the IB has enhanced my time-management and organizational skills. Another vital skill that I have been taught through this Program is the Extended Essay. Having selected a particularly engaging topic, "To what extent has American cinematography reflected and shaped social attitudes towards mental illness?" I developed my critical thinking skills and was made fully aware of what a university education will entail.

It is my firm belief that a good educator must be a versatile individual with knowledge of a wide range of subjects. I have endeavored to broaden my horizons through several activities. For instance, classical ballet taught me discipline and dedication to something I love. Furthermore, practicing the piano enabled me to realize how important a role music can play in education. I participated in the Student UNESCO Symposium in 2012, which was entitled "The Transformation of the World". This experience gave me the opportunity to become aware of the global aspect of education and to exchange views pertaining to the topic with my peers.

I am very familiar with the organization and structure of British Universities having attended several summer courses at British Universities and I am confident that, given the opportunity, I will be able to make the most of my studies in the UK and make a valuable contribution to the shaping of children's future through education. There is no doubt in my mind that Britain is the place, where a sound educational basis can be formed on which to build for the future.

<u>Example 3:</u> (2009: Applicant for Chemistry)

Few aspects of life fall outside the scope of chemistry, and this is what fascinates me about this dynamic and fundamental science subject. From a young age I have enjoyed and excelled in mathematics which reflects my logical and enquiring mind. Thus, I made the decision at high school to study mathematics as well as two sciences as part of the International Baccalaureate. It was during this part of my education that I discovered my interest in Chemistry and my desire to study the subject at a higher level. Furthermore, I developed an enthusiasm for the topics of energetics and in particular, organics.

My practical skills have been greatly enhanced through the study of Biology and Chemistry and the assessment of my abilities. Earlier this year I completed the Group 4 Project, which required me to utilize many life skills as well as calling on the skills learnt in my two science subjects. The Group 4 Project consists of a group of 8 students formulating a research question, planning, and executing relevant experiments and finally drawing and presenting conclusions. Good teamwork and practical skills were a must, and I was pleased to be awarded very high marks. My love for chemistry stems from an appetite to understand the physical world around me and learn about, what is sometimes referred to as the central science.

The subjects I study at standard level differ greatly from my higher and subsequently they have enabled me to broaden my knowledge. This is partly the reason I chose the IB. Another salient reason as to why I chose to take the IB was because of the opportunities the course offered through the inner hexagon. My studies of Theory of Knowledge have helped me to evolve an analytical and questioning mind which I feel is very applicable in the ever-expanding field of modern chemistry. The IB is a very challenging course, but I feel it has strengthened me in many aspects.

Since starting the course in September of 2007 I have enhanced my time management and organizational skills in addition to becoming a more open minded and reflective person. Recently I have written and submitted a 3700-word extended essay about the area of circles and formulation of Pi, requiring me to exercise both my research and essay writing ability.

Presently I am working towards achieving my Duke of Edinburgh Gold Award and during my Easter holiday last year, I travelled to South Wales in the company of a group of 6 friends with the ambition of qualifying for the final assessed expedition. I believe that I showed great determination over the four days walking as well as overcoming the challenge of being self-sufficient. My other pastimes include trampolining, playing the bass guitar and practicing parkour. I love being involved in sport and through parkour I can show self-expression, control, and discipline.

A level of self-confidence, an ambitious mind, and a hardworking attitude towards improving are all qualities I feel parkour has helped me to achieve. Over the year and 6 months I have attended the Sixth Form I have completed over 150 CAS hours by recording my past times and charity work in a fair-trade coffee shop. Parallel to my studies, I enjoy working as a waiter in a local hotel. This involves me being punctual, hardworking, sociable and most of all, responsible for my own thinking and acting upon this. These are all skills that I believe are vital for any perspective university student. I am greatly looking forward to the opportunities that university has to offer me both academically and socially.

My passion for Chemistry, determination and positive attitude lead me to the conclusion that studying a course at university that will both excite me and satisfy my thirst for knowledge, such as chemistry, is the next step for me and my education. My eventual aim is to become a teacher of Chemistry at GCSE level and to inject the excitement into the subject that I have discovered.

<u>Example 4:</u> (2019: Applicant for Liberal Arts)

As a child I disliked reading; however, when I was 8, there was one particular book that caught my attention: The Little Prince. From that moment onwards, my love for literature was ignited and I had entered into a whirlwind of fictional worlds. While studying and analyzing the classics from The Great Gatsby to Candide, this has exposed me to a variety of novels. My French bilingualism allowed me to study, in great depth, different texts in their original language. This sparked a new passion of mine for poetry, and introduced me to the works of Arthur Rimbaud, who has greatly influenced me. Through both reading and analyzing poetry I was able to decipher its meaning. Liberal Arts gives me the opportunity to continue to study a range of texts and authors from different periods in history, as well as related aspects of culture, economy, and society.

[Here we have a slightly longer than usual opening paragraph but, given the nature of the course being applied for, this works well. A personal story segueing from literature to modern languages to history and cultural studies shows that this student has a broad range of interests within the humanities and thus is well-suited to this course of study.]

Liberal Arts is a clear choice for me. Coming from the IB International Baccalaureate Diploma program I have studied a wide range of subjects which has provided me with a breadth of knowledge. In Theatre, I have adapted classics such as Othello by Shakespeare, and playing the role of moreover acting as Desdemona forced me to compartmentalize her complex emotions behind the early-modern English text. Studying History has taught me a number of skills, understanding the reasons behind changes in society, evaluating sources, and considering conflicting interpretations. From my interdisciplinary education I can critically analyze the world around me. Through studying Theory of Knowledge, I have developed high quality analysis using key questions and a critical mindset by questioning how and why we think and why. By going beyond the common use of reason, I have been able to deepen greaten my understanding and apply my ways of knowing in all subjects; for example, in science I was creative in constructing my experiment (imagination) and used qualitative data (sense perception).

[Remember that students who are taking the IB Diploma, with its structure to retain a broad curriculum, are well-suited to the UK's Liberal Arts courses, as they have had practice seeing the links between subjects. In this paragraph, the applicant shows how she has done this, linking content from one subject to skills developed in another, and touching on the experience of IB Theory of Knowledge (an interdisciplinary class compulsory for all IB Diploma students) to show how she is able to see how different academic subjects overlap and share some common themes.]

Languages have always played an important role in my life. I was immersed into a French nursery even though my parents are not French speakers. I have always cherished the ability to speak another language; it is something I have never taken for granted, and it is how I individualize myself. Being bilingual has allowed me to engage with a different culture. As a result, I am more open minded and have a global outlook. This has fueled my desire to travel, learn new languages and experience new cultures. This course would provide me with the opportunity to fulfil these desires. Having written my Extended Essay in French on the use of manipulative language used by a particular character from the French classic Dangerous Liaisons I have had to apply my skills of close contextual reading and analyzing to sculpt this essay. These skills are perfectly applicable to the critical thinking that is demanded for the course.

[Within the humanities, this student has a particular background that makes her stand out, having become fluent in French while having no French background nor living in a French-speaking country. This is worth her exploring to develop her motivation for a broad course of study at university, which she does well here.]

Studying the Liberal Arts will allow me to further my knowledge in a variety of fields whilst living independently and meeting people from different backgrounds. The flexible skills I would achieve from obtaining a liberal arts degree I believe would make me more desirable for future employment. I would thrive in this environment due to my self-discipline and determination. During my school holidays I have undertaken working in a hotel as a chambermaid and this has made me appreciate the service sector in society and has taught me to work cohesively with others in an unfamiliar environment. I also took part in a creative writing course held at Keats House, where I learnt about romanticism. My commitment to extracurricular activities such as varsity football and basketball has shown me the importance of sportsmanship and camaraderie, while

GIN (Global Issue Networking) has informed me of the values of community and the importance for charitable organizations.

[The extracurricular paragraph here draws out a range of skills the student will apply to this course. Knowing that taking a broader range of subjects at a UK university requires excellent organizational skills, the student takes time to explain how she can meet these, perhaps going into slightly more detail than would be necessary for a single-honors application to spell out that she is capable of managing her time well. She then broadens this at the end by touching on some activities that have relevance for her studies.]

My academic and personal preferences have always led me to the Liberal Arts; I feel as though the International Baccalaureate, my passion and self-discipline have prepared me for higher education. From the academics, extracurriculars and social aspects, I intend to embrace the entire experience of university.

Example 5: (Applicant for Law, 2019)

Conflict is a dominant feature of our society, and I view law as a means to accommodate and arbitrate differing interests. Legislation on even seemingly minor matters, such as parking regulations, must balance competing interests – here, the rights of different groups to use the road. I wish to study law to develop my ability to critically evaluate discordant viewpoints, deepening my understanding and capacity to resolve some of the bitter disputes of our world.

Law's role in resolving conflict is most evident in court, seen in the case Comcare v PVYW. When I initially read about the disagreement over the compensation paid to an employee injured whilst engaging in sexual activities on a work trip, I dismissed the newspaper story as sensationalizing the trivial. Several years later, however, I observed this case's appeal in the High Court of Australia. I witnessed the conflict over whether the worker's injury was sustained "in the course of employment", which would justify compensation. There was lengthy debate on whether a temporal connection between employment and injury was sufficient, or whether a causal link had to be proved. This deepened my respect for the law in constructing detailed, sophisticated arguments and drawing upon prior legal judgements to defend a view.

By partaking in Model United Nations events as a national finalist, I developed an interest in emerging international legal norms such as the "responsibility to protect". When researching, amending, and negotiating mock resolutions as a Russian delegate, I cautioned against the abuse of "responsibility to protect" in justifying Western military intervention and infringement of sovereignty upon the pretext of protecting civilian rights. However, I personally feel that when mass atrocity crimes such as genocide are confirmed, its impacts are so horrendous that foreign nations should intervene through a variety of measures. I wish to further study international law as an incipient attempt to balance civilian and national interests.

Studying English Literature and History in the International Baccalaureate Diploma developed my ability to closely and critically analyze written evidence to support theses. In Physics and Mathematics Higher Level, I strengthened my capacity to logically construct arguments and make conclusions, critical to forming and justifying legal arguments.

School and community activities have also instilled in me a desire to help others, which I hope to further by understanding law as an arbitrator of divisive conflicts. In adjudicating school debating, tutoring younger peers, and acting as piano accompanist at chapel services, I have shared my time and skills to benefit others. This is also evident in my role as a Senior Prefect and an organizer of school charity events.

I also participated in the 2013 National Schools Debating Championships, as part of the winning NSW team. I refined my ability to argue persuasively, with rhetorical logic and manner, as well as my collaborative skills. Participating in state-level public speaking competitions, I developed my capacity to select evidence to support strong stances on international issues, valuable to a law student in justifying a particular interpretation of a legal statement. By studying law, I hope to enhance my ability to advocate and critique competing viewpoints, furthering myself in the aim of comprehending and resolving conflicts in our society.

Example 6: (Applicant for History)

History's appeal to me lies in the complexity of the relationships between people and ideas that have driven society's development. These relationships are seen not only in history but also historiography: the origins and effects of an event can lead to a substantial amount of unique interpretations. Considering how a historian's research may have been affected by their own views, and lately reading works on historiography, has made my fascination with the subject deeper than just intellectual curiosity on historical events. In this way history has made me more aware of my own views and biases as they affect the way I interpret the past as well as the way I see the world.

One of my historical interests is single-party states and dictatorships. I have broadened my knowledge of this topic by reading not only works on individual nations but also fictional dystopian novels. "The Third Reich: A New History", by Michael Burleigh, is a very fascinating moral history of Nazi Germany. Burleigh's comparison between religion and political ideology was especially interesting considering the centrality of religion as an instrument of earlier political control. This cult hypothesis also seemed to partly answer the question of why the opposition to Nazi rule was fairly limited. In addition, I enjoyed Hannah Arendt's sharp analysis on the emergence and functions of totalitarian states in "Origins of Totalitarianism". Although in some ways a work of political science, I found the book as a whole extremely thought-provoking and helpful for my studies in history as it provided a comparative framework for the discussion of several totalitarian nations.

My IB coursework, a historical investigation on the motives for Caesar's assassination, allowed me to consider dictatorships in a rather different, unfamiliar context. A more extensive project was my Extended Essay work. Due to my particular interest in the Cold War years in Finland and the continuous Russian influence on the nation's history, I chose to research how the country's foreign policy of Finlandization affected Finnish history textbooks in years 1970-79. Both of these works improved my skills in research and individual study, and I greatly enjoyed the research process of my Extended Essay which required in-depth study of the contemporary Finnish political climate and heavy reliance on primary sources.

My interest in political history has led me to take part in European Youth Parliament sessions, and I was given the opportunity to attend an International Session in October 2010. Working effectively with ten young people from differing backgrounds to consider political issues such as multiculturalism has developed my teamwork skills and clear argumentation. My positions of responsibility include the vice chairmanship of the nationwide Finnish International Baccalaureate Organization, as well as of one of the ten regional branches of The Union for Finnish Upper Secondary School Students. These positions, along with academic commitments, have required responsibility and time management, but I have also enjoyed them greatly. I have organized events such as an annual seminar cruise with 400 attendees and been able to defend students' rights such as equal treatment in university admissions for IB students. I am planning to continue similar activities in university.

In my spare time I play classical piano and keep up on current affairs from both domestic and foreign news sources. I am also an avid reader: besides works related to history I like authors such as Gustav Flaubert and Emily Bronte. One of my main characteristics is my affection for learning, and I strive to become a lifelong learner. A degree in history, a discipline that I love, is the best possible foundation for that.

Example 7: (Applicant for Politics)

Although I was too young to remember or understand the significance of the break-up of the Soviet Union and the demolition of the Berlin Wall I was harshly introduced to the world of politics when... [Information removed to respect the student's privacy].

Naturally, this family episode stimulated my interest in the events of that period and when I got older, I was fascinated to read about it and previous periods of Russian and world history. At the age of 13 I attended an international boarding school and was able to have access to English language books on history and politics. This was a major eye opener for me as I realized that the same events can be shown in a very different light depending on who is writing about them. The more I read, the more I began to understand the importance of international relations in the global economy and the more I observed my President's political aspirations the more I understood that politics is the study of power.

As my studies progressed in the IB Diploma Program, I was able to add Economics to History as Higher-Level subjects, and this complemented my understanding of important historical events such as the Great Depression and the forced industrialization of the Soviet Union. What has greatly impressed me is that my knowledge of history, economics and politics allows me to understand issues which were previously unfamiliar to me, such as the Arab-Israeli conflict and the involvement of the Soviet Union and now The USA and Britain in Afghanistan.

I eventually want to follow a career in politics and hope that as a post-Soviet person I will be able to offer a fresh approach and help to replace corruption and nepotism with a system based on merit and the rule of law. This might sound naïve and pretentious but as a young person I have to try to make a difference and stand up for my beliefs like some brave people in Russia are doing.

In order to pursue my passion for international relations, I participated in Model United Nations, which gave me a chance to take part in 3 conferences, in different parts of the world. It was captivating to be involved with international students my age, engaging into academic debates about global issues, and coming up with solutions to on-going conflicts, and crisis. The MUN conference hosted by Harvard in Beijing particularly had a significant impact on my view of the world politics. As it was the first occasion on which I have encountered political views of Asian students and heard their priorities in Global concerns. I found out about their main worries for the future of our world, and their attitudes towards globalization, poverty, and international diplomacy. After this experience I was able to make more connections between attitudes from all regions and add key pieces to the puzzle of global politics.

In addition, I have gained some work experience in the Russian Senate in the department of foreign affairs, where I took part in organizing a Russian-Chinese Business and Economics summit that took place in Omsk, Siberia in October 2013. It was a very educational experience as I witnessed the negotiations process and learnt about organization of official events according to the protocol.

I have also done an internship, during the Festival of Russian Culture in France, which was hosted by the Russian Ministry of Culture. During this experience I learnt about different cultures and attitudes, and I also improved my translating skills, in French, English and Russian. As a result of these two experiences, I now have a much better insight into the distinctive cultural characteristics of different countries.

Pro Tip: let everyone around you proofread your final PS draft - but don't post it online or email to anyone you don't know.

This Personal Statement is very interesting because it uses a strong personal experience to show the applicant's deep interest in the subject. Personal stories that are truly powerful and genuine can make your statement very strong, so if you have one - use it.

However, the average student will not have such a fascinating story. If you don't, no worries. Just explain why you are interested in the course rather than trying to exaggerate personal experiences.

Pro Tip: Do not put off writing your personal statement until the last moment!

CHAPTER 4

UNITED KINGDOM

IBO Information

We will begin each chapter with some relevant information found in official IBO documentation[10]. For example, here is some of their advice from their student guide on UK applications:[11]

The UK context

The UK includes the countries of England, Scotland, Wales, and Northern Ireland. There are more than 160 universities and colleges in the UK, offering a variety of options for students pursuing degrees in higher education. This guide provides information primarily for those applying to degree-granting universities. However, attending a degree-granting university, a listed body or pursuing a career after completing the IB Diploma Program are all viable options.

---

[10] **See** https://blogs.ibo.org/blog/2016/04/07/student-guides-for-applying-to-university-abroad/
[11] **Adapted from** https://www.ibo.org/contentassets/5895a05412144fe890312bad52b17044/recognition---international-student-guide-uk--march2016---eng.pdf.pdf

Listed Bodies

There are more than 700 colleges and other institutions known as "listed bodies" that do not grant degrees but offer courses that could lead to a degree at a degree-granting university. These listed bodies each have their own application system.

Degree length

The same government regulations and processes apply to all four countries in the UK, so the application process for universities and colleges is consistent throughout. However, Scotland has a different system of education from the others, so there are important differences to note. Most degrees in the UK can be completed in three years, but Scottish courses of study typically take four years. A "sandwich year" is becoming more popular in UK universities, in which students spend one year (usually their third) in the workplace before returning to the university to finish their degrees.

UK University Attitudes to the DP

British universities have a very positive attitude to DP applicants as IB students have developed a broad range of skills and so are prepared for higher education. The recently published HESA report comparing IB and A Level students' outcomes in higher education clearly demonstrates that IB students make excellent progress at university. In particular, this report shows:

- That between 2012 and 2013, 46 percent of DP students achieved places to study at a top 20 UK university compared to 33 percent of A Level students.
- DP students have a greater likelihood of earning a first-class honors degree compared to their A Level peers (23 percent versus 19 percent respectively).

- Of the students who successfully complete a full-time undergraduate degree at a UK university, DP students are significantly more likely to be engaged in further study, while A Level students are more likely to join the workforce at this point.

Heads of Admissions from top UK universities have said the following about the DP:

"We welcome applications from students following the International Baccalaureate Diploma Program. Most degree courses offered at Bristol require a point score of at least 32 with some requirements as high as 38 points, with 18 points at higher level. Where specified subjects are required at A Level, we may specify 6 points at HL for grade A* or A, and 5 points at higher level for grade B." - *University of Bristol*

"King's welcomes students from the UK and across the globe studying the IB Diploma. Our offers will usually specify certain marks in three subjects at higher level, in addition to an overall point score for the whole Diploma. Our point score includes points for Theory of Knowledge and the Extended Essay." - *King's College, London*

"We welcome applications from IB students. Our offers are based on your overall IB score, but we may also require specific grades in relevant higher-level subjects. Our course pages give full details of the grades and subjects required. Our typical offer ranges from 31-36." - *University of York*

These examples prove selective universities make offers based on the total points achieved by the applicant as well as attainment in the higher-level subjects.

Tariff System

UCAS has a well-known 'tariff' system to enable qualifications to be compared. Most institutions receiving applications from IB students, however, do not use the UCAS tariff in their application procedures; UCAS estimates that the tariff is only used in about 30 percent of IB applications. The current tariff allocates points for the total IB score, or for the individual subjects if a student has not completed the full DP.

As of 2017, a revised UCAS tariff system has been implemented, in a change of approach allocating points to the subjects that comprise the DP. Note that even if a university makes an offer based on the tariff, it may stipulate that the points should be from a specific combination of Diploma courses.

Parents and students sometimes ask what the A Level equivalent of an IB points score is. This is difficult as it is not comparing like with like. A Level outcomes are usually based on 3 A Levels, whereas the DP is a 5 A Level equivalent program with prescribed elements.

For a number of years, the Higher Education Funding Council (HEFCE) has defined a 'good pass' as consisting of ABB for A Level students and 34 points for IB students, in order to exempt students from student number controls.

Some examples of IB offers from a range of universities are:

University	Course	Entrance offer
University of Oxford	English	38 points + 666 at higher level
University of Cambridge	Natural Sciences	40 points + 776 at higher level
Kings College London	Medicine	35 points + 666 at higher level
Bristol University	Math	38 points + 66 at higher level
Durham University	Law	36 points + 666 at higher level
University College London	History	39 points + 19 at higher level
Leeds University	International Business	35 points + 17 at higher level
Nottingham University	Geography	34 points + 5 at higher level

Many UK universities vary their offers depending on the subject being applied for, e.g., Exeter University requires 34 for Biology, 36 for Psychology and 38 for Economics. However, a number of universities have taken the initiative to request the same points total for all subjects, tempered by differences in the points for higher level. Currently, these universities are:

- Birmingham University 32 total points
- Royal Holloway College, London 32 total points
- University of Kent, 34 total points
- University of Leeds, 35 total points
- Kings College, London 35 total points
- University of Bath, 36 total points

UCAS

The application process in the UK is typically done through the UK's centralized admissions body, the Universities and Colleges Admissions Service (UCAS). Students fill out one form, upload a personal statement and include one reference. Their school should submit their IB predicted grades. Students then identify up to five courses to which they would like to apply (four in the case of clinical programs such as medicine or dentistry). The five courses can be at five different universities, or students can apply to two or more courses at the same university.

Most schools provide assistance to their applicants so that the majority apply through the school supported option. This involves a school faculty member tasked with writing a reference for the student. However, it is also possible for the student to apply individually and to request a reference from someone who is not affiliated with student's school.[12]

STEP 1: Registration on the UCAS website

The firsts step involves filling in some personal information (name, address, etc.) as well as entering your email and password (please try to use a professional school-administered email, and not spongebobxx08@hotmail.com). A verification code will then be sent to you and with this you should be able to log onto your application form using the ID provided and your password.

STEP 2: Logging on

Your school should provide you with a buzzword that will be used when logging on. Different parts of the application form will now be accessible to you. The first section will be your personal details (some of which you have already filled in). You should then proceed to fill out and complete this section and then click 'section completed'. Your information is continuously saved - and you can always return and edit this in case you entered something wrong or if your information changes. The remaining sections in the UCAS form will then be:

- Choices
- Education
- Employment
- Personal Statement
- References

---

[12] For example, this may happen if the student has already graduated and decides to apply at a later date.

STEP 3: Filling in the information

Education

Aside from the references and choices (which we will deal with in the following section), you can now proceed to fill in the sections in any order.

Beginning with education, you will be requested to enter all previous schools that you have attended in recent years as well as any official exams and where you will be completing your IB Diploma examinations.

Pro Tip: The potentially tricky part here is to register your qualifications in chronological order and make sure that the dates match up with a school that you attended at that date.

This is in order to streamline the application process and to register mainstream qualifications such as IGCSE, IELTS, Cambridge proficiency, etc.

European applicants, however, may find it difficult to find the relevant language qualifications (such as Delf, Dalf A1 for French applicants). These should be listed as 'other' on the dropdown box. The process is similar for national equivalents to the GCSE examinations. If it is not officially listed, you should include your national/local qualifications using the 'other' box (but make sure to include them!).

Pro Tip: Make sure that you carefully check the list of qualifications because you might forget to record a music or dance or language certificate that you have worked hard to obtain!

It cannot be emphasized enough that one of the most important selection criteria that admissions officers are looking at is *evidence of academic ability.* This is why you need to include as much of this evidence as possible. Indeed, actual obtained grades are far more convincing to them than predicted grades.

IB Subjects

After you have entered all the qualifications that you have obtained, you will need to fill in all your IB subjects or certificates that you will be completing. Please remember to include the EE and TOK along with your 6 'subjects'. In the results box, you should enter 'pending'.

You should also enter any other qualifications, such as language exams, SAT, AP, etc. that you plan on completing before graduating. Please ensure that the date you will be taking these exams corresponds to a date that you will be in attendance at the school/ educational establishment in this section. Otherwise, you may risk confusing UCAS and will not be able to enter the subject.

Employment

The following section deals with employment. Do not freak out! You do not need to feel frightened by this section and feel like you should have something to enter here. Even when I was applying for my 2nd masters at the ripe age of 22, I still did not have any real work experience - so nobody really expects 16- and 17-year-olds to have held previous jobs. This section is mainly for applicants who have worked after leaving school and who have then decided to apply to university. It also applies to alumni who have taken a gap year in order to gain work experience.

Pro Tip: It's OK to take a gap year - don't feel pressure to start university immediately. Your life is literally **just starting** so don't stress and do things at your own pace.

For the typical IB student who is still completing high school, there is absolutely zero expectation of having employment experience.

Some applicants may choose to enter part-time employment or summer jobs they have held (although this can also be mentioned in the personal statement).

Pro Tip: Leaving this section blank will in no way harm your application! However, if you do indeed have some relevant work experience, you should list it here along with your employer's contact details in the rare instance that the university wishes to contact them.

The value of any employment experience is with respect to the benefit it provides and how it affects your suitability to the course you are choosing. Therefore, if it is to be useful to your application, it needs to be discussed in your personal statement also.

Submitting the Application

When your application is completed, it will be sent to UCAS after you or your school has paid the application fee. UCAS will then send off a copy of your form to each of your chosen universities. When the university receives your form, it will have no information about your other choices but simply knows that you have applied to that university for that specific course. On the receipt of your application, most universities will acknowledge this by communicating to you by email.

UCAS also sends an acknowledgement by post which may include a possibly revised application number. This number, coupled with your password, allows you to log in and 'track' your application so that you can follow the progress of your application. To do so will require that you click on 'choices' and it is here where any information regarding the status of your application will be shown.

In the event that an offer of a place has been made, this will be indicated and the conditions of the offer together with a letter can be accessed. If the university course does not give you an offer, this will be indicated as 'unsuccessful' (basically, a nice way of saying you got rejected). When all decisions have been made from all of your choices, you will be given a date by which you have to reply.

You are requested to accept one of your offers as a 'firm choice', one as an 'insurance' and then decline the remaining choices. It makes sense that the most preferred offer is your 'firm', and the less preferred and 2nd choice is your 'insurance'. It is normal for the university to notify applicants of a decision and for UCAS to do so likewise. Normally, you will receive an update that the status of your application has changed.

Pro Tip: You are nonetheless advised to regularly track your application for updates. Friday evenings has, traditionally, been the most frequent time for changes in decision.

After you make your decision, you will need to wait for your results in order to see if you have met the conditions of the offer.

It is here that IB applicants have a significant advantage over A-level students because IB results usually come out in the first week of July, whereas A-Level results are usually published around the 15th of August. This means that successful applicant can confirm their places early and proceed to make arrangements regarding accommodation and travel.

Pro Tip: If a student narrowly misses the conditions of their offer, the university may nevertheless be willing to confirm a place depending on the number of successful IB applicants and past experiences.

Unfortunately, most of the time even if you fail to meet an offer, you will need to wait until A-Level results come out before the university can decide.

Pro Tip: If you missed your offer, we nonetheless **strongly recommend contacting the university to** see what your prospects are (usually calling the admission office to explain your situation).

You may also indicate to them that you plan to appeal for a re-mark if it is one subject where you missed out on. This is exactly what I had to do when I first got my results and got a 6 in HL Math (but needed a 7 - and I was very close to the boundary). I explained that there was a slight chance my IA mark would increase, and lo and behold, that's exactly what happened. If possible, please ask for your school and your coordinator to assist you in these negotiations.

For more information of whether you should appeal an exam result and ask for a remark, please consult the document 'The Complete Guide to IB Results' (google that term and you should find it - it is made possible by the IB Students Worldwide Facebook group).

Pro Tip: Always have a good fallback option. You never know what might happen.

References

The last section in the UCAS form is the references, which need to be completed by someone who is very familiar with your academic potential and performance, as well as your suitability for the degree you are applying to. The vast majority of IB applications go through their respective IB schools, so the referee is almost always a teacher or counsellor who has some good experience and knowledge in this area.

The person responsible will usually collect information from your teachers and collate this to form an overall opinion regarding your academic performances to date, your predicted grades, your contributions to the school community and your suitability for the chosen course of study.

Pro Tip: It is not the end of the world if your predicted grades are not that great. We'd all like to go to Oxbridge - but not all of us can. Don't let these things put you down and have faith in yourself!

As an IB student, you do not really have any *direct* influence on what will be written by your referee (although I have seen some students on such good terms with their teachers, that they get to read a draft before it's submitted!) However, you can substantially improve your profile by performing well in mock exams and by showing a willingness to participate in school and CAS activities. Some diplomatic skills are also necessary in order to secure the most positive and encouraging references. For more detailed information on how to get on your teacher's good side, I suggest reading the chapter 'How To Win Friends And Influence Teachers' from *The Secret Art of Passing the IB Diploma* (Zouev, 2019)

Pro Tip: Be warned! Most teachers will get ticked off and upset if you constantly pester them about your predicted grades. If you want a favorable predictions and references, just make sure to do your work on time and meet all the IB deadlines.

It is absolutely imperative that the person who you choose to write your reference is someone who is not only highly literate, but more importantly can fill the reference full of praise and admiration. Obviously, the person writing your reference should be closely related to the subject you intend to study at university. There are minor exceptions to this.

For example, when I was applying to study economics, my economics teacher at school did not necessarily dislike me, however I did feel that they would not put all of their efforts into writing a stand-out reference and perhaps it would not be as elegantly written. Instead, I sought the help of my geography teacher (who happened to hold a PhD from LSE and had previously taught economics and business at a high school level).

The teacher in question clearly saw a lot of potential in me, so I asked for help and got a wonderfully written reference in return. Whoever you seek for this task, make sure they are not going to write a generic reference but instead something personal and something that will make you stand out.

Ideally, the reference should complement your personal statement. Therefore, it is advisable for applicants to competitive courses, who have the necessary academic credentials, to work closely with their referee in order to decide what to include in the personal statement and what to mention in the reference.

Keep in mind that schools gain prestige if their students get offers from competitive universities but also lose prestige if they fail to achieve the offer. You and your school need to be realistic about your opportunities and potential. If you are deemed to be a valid applicant for a highly competitive course, you need to work closely with your referee to present your application in the most favorable light possible.

Pro Tip: You should ensure that your school supports your course choices and that your predicted grades are appropriate for the courses and universities to which you are applying. If a course requires a 7 in HL Physics but your teacher has only predicted you a 4 or 5, then including it would be a waste.

If you genuinely feel that your school is underestimating your qualities and abilities, you may try to convey this in the personal statement (covered in the next section).

Lastly, too many students do not consider the importance of the reference. Keep in mind that top universities want to know that you are a person who is passionate about their studies and can cope well with a university workload. They will trust the words of your teachers/superiors more than anything else.

You must ensure that you seek out the best possible faculty member to write your reference and you must ensure that they do the best that they can.

Important Dates

(Please note that the following information is for 2022 entry)

18 May 2021

UCAS Undergraduate application opens for 2022 entry.

7 September 2021

Applicants can pay and send their applications to UCAS, and universities and colleges can start making decisions on applications.

15 October 2021

Applications for Oxford, Cambridge and most courses in medicine, dentistry, and veterinary medicine/science should arrive at UCAS by 18:00 (UK time). The reference needs to be completed before the application can be sent.

Pro Tip: In order to meet the deadline, it is necessary to complete your sections of the form well before this date in order to give your referee enough time to write your reference!

More information on Oxbridge applications will be covered in later sections.

26 January 2022

Applications for the majority of undergraduate courses should arrive at UCAS by 18:00 (UK time) on the equal consideration date. The reference needs to be completed before the application can be sent.

It is **always advisable to apply well before this deadline**. If you are applying to competitive courses, but not to Oxbridge or Medicine, it is advisable to send your application towards the end of October or early November. If your application is strong, there is a good chance you may even receive an offer before the Christmas break! (I think I got mine around Dec 15th).

Some universities will look at applications as they come in and like to send out replies as they go along, while others wait until all the applications are in before making decisions. Either way, all of your choices are obliged to reply to you by the end of March or some other specified date (e.g., if you use 'extra' or apply after the January deadline).

Note here that even though the closing date for applications is 15th January, many universities will accept applications even after this date.

Pro Tip: The most competitive ('best') Russel Group[13] courses will not usually accept late applications!

25 February 2022

Extra starts for eligible applicants.

If, for whatever reason, you later decide to add a choice or apply after the deadline, you should check that the university is willing to consider late applications. A good indicator of this is whether the course is available on 'extra'. An extra listing means that the course is open for applications and is available for applicants who have been unsuccessful with all their applications.

---

[13] The Russell Group is a self-selected association of twenty-four universities in the United Kingdom. Its members are sometimes perceived as being the most prestigious universities in the country. See https://en.wikipedia.org/wiki/Russell_Group for more information.

30 June 2022

The start of Clearing.

Applications received after this date will automatically be entered into Clearing.

Pro Tip: Apply early! Don't let those deadlines look over your and continuously stress you out... if you get it out of the way, you can focus on your IAs and IB work.

I planned everything over the summer of IBY1 to IBY2. I highly recommend you also do this. You can enjoy your summer but spend some time thinking ahead.

Clearing

The clearing process begins a few days after the publication of A-Level. If you have not had confirmation of a place by this time, you will be eligible to enter 'clearing'. The aim is to find a course that interests you and which is willing to offer you a place with the grades that you have.

If you find yourself in this situation, you should get online and check various websites which list available courses. The best advice here is to make a list of telephone numbers for the courses that interest you and contact them by phone to see if they are willing to accept you.

Pro Tip: If you call up the university's admission office, you need to make absolutely sure that the person you are speaking to knows that you are **an IB student!** And more importantly, that they are actually familiar with the IB grading system (because most of the calls they receive are from A-Level students).

If your grades are acceptable, you will be able to apply for the course on UCAS using your clearing number to secure your place. The university will then notify you that you have been accepted and informed of the dates for registration.

In order to register for the course, you will have to make arrangement for payment of fees, and you will be required to provide proof of your qualifications that meet the conditions of the offer. The main document will be the IB Diploma, but you should also have any other certificates that might be relevant.

Most universities will then invite new students to an introductory week ('Freshers Week' as it is more commonly known) where you will get to know your new classmates (and have a bunch of drunken fun)! Once you have gotten to this stage, you can put this book away and officially begin your university experience.

Understanding Offers

Offers will be 'conditional' unless you already have all of the qualifications that you are going to present, in which case you will either receive an 'unconditional' offer or a rejection.

A conditional offer will specify the conditions with respect to the IB Diploma score that is required together with any other pending qualification. The conditions will vary from university to university and across courses, depending on how competitive the course is and how the IB is perceived.

A typical offer will include an overall IB Diploma score together with specific subject scores.

For example, you may get the following offer:

> **38** points overall with **7, 6, 6 at Higher Level**
> and no subject below **5.**

More competitive courses (like Economics and Management at Oxford, or Economics at LSE) will usually require a 7 in HL Math.

Usually, universities include the bonus points (for EE and TOK) in the overall score. However sometimes they might exclude them or only include 1 of the 3 bonus points. For example, City University gives a typical offer for Business and Management of 35 but only includes 1 bonus point in this total.

Choosing Your Degree

Most people start to look for university places begin by choosing a subject and course, rather than a university. If you take a degree, then you should be prepared to be fully immersed in your subject for at least three years. It has to be one you will enjoy and can master - not to mention, one that you are qualified to study. Many economics degrees require math, for example, while some medical schools demand chemistry or biology. The UCAS website contains course profiles, including entrance requirements, which is a good starting point, while universities own sites contain more detailed information.

The official yardstick by which your IB result will be judged is the UCAS tariff which gives a score for each point total received. There has been some controversy in recent years about how the points are worked out and the discrepancies between A-Levels and the IB program. Top scores in the new vocational diplomas in A-Levels, for example will attract more points than a full set of A grades at A level, while the most successful IB students already earn considerably more points. If this process continues it is likely that more of the leading universities will abandon the tariff as some have done already.

Choosing your subject at university is not always as straightforward as it sounds. Your IB subjects may have chosen themselves, but the range of subjects across the whole university system is vast. Even subjects that you have studied at school may be quite different at degree level - some academic economists actually prefer their undergraduates not to have taken IB economics because they approach the subject so differently. Indeed, this was the case for when I applied to study Economics and Management at Oxford. Another scenario is that students are disappointed because they appear to be going over old ground when they continue with a subject that they enjoyed at school. Universities now publish quite detailed syllabuses, and you should go through these very carefully.

If you are not sure whether you will be suited to a particular subject, you can take an online aptitude test through the UCAS website. The 'What to study' section gives you access to the Stamford Test, which uses an online questionnaire to match your interests and strengths to possible courses and careers.

You may find that more than one subject appeals to you, in which case you could consider Joint Honors - degrees that combine two subjects - or even Combined Honors, which will cover several related subjects. Such courses obviously allow you to extend the scope of your studies, but they should be approached with caution. Even if the number of credits suggests a similar workload to Single Honors, covering more than one subject inevitably involves extra reading and often more essays or project work. The advantages are quite obvious. Many students choose a 'dual' degree to add a vocational element and make themselves more employable - business studies with languages or engineering for example, or media studies with English. Others want to take their studies in a particular direction, perhaps by combining history with politics, or statistics with math. Some simply want to add a completely unrelated interest to their main subject such as archaeology and event management.

Personally, however, I feel that your university course choice needs to be a combination of a few factors but most importantly you need to have a somewhat clear picture of what you intend to do with your degree. It is not wise to have a career mapped out as an investment banker and for that reason alone try to get into an economics course at a top university. You should have some passion and interest in the course that you wish to study. At the same time, if you wish to become a dentist or something very specific, taking a course in design or art will do you no good.

For me, the choice to study economics was a rather simple one. I enjoyed math a lot throughout high school, and my father put a certain emphasis on doing well in both mathematics and economics because, in his words, 'it will be important for your future, regardless of what career you choose'. Although that may not be necessarily true, I did have a feeling I would end up an investment banker or working somewhere within the realms of finance. Also, given the fact that my brother had just graduated with a degree in Economics from Cambridge and had only good things to say, I was left with little choice but to follow in his footsteps.

Pro Tip: Research, research, and more research! A failure to do this will cause unnecessary anxiety. There is no worse feeling than realizing you chose the wrong options because of lack of preparation and poor research.

You should certainly devote a significant portion of time prior to filling out your UCAS form to researching the specifics of various courses. And when I say specifics, I mean specifics. Start by browsing the websites and see if there are any timetables or course-specific materials available to the public. If not, email the departments and express your interest in applying and finding out more information. Last but not least, we live in such an interconnected world where you can find alumni from specific courses with a click of a button. Utilize Facebook and websites like studentroom.co.uk to find graduates and ask them any questions you may have.

The times are constantly changing, and whereas a few years ago a degree in 'business and management' may have been seen as the must-have diploma, many would argue that this is no longer the case. Perhaps we have reached a point where there are 'too many' business degrees available and not enough traditional and vocational applicants. I would not be surprised to see a turnaround and more students applying to become doctors or lawyers in the next few decades. Although you are only in your late teens, you should have some idea already of what you wish to become - and this should help guide your university course choice.

Making your choices

You can select up to **five** courses on the UCAS application. Do note here that it is possible that you might wish to apply to two or more courses from the *same university.* This will be the case if you like a particular university which has more than one course that interests you. For example, a university that offers both an Economics course and also a Management course - and you would be interested in applying to both.

> **Pro Tip:** If applying for multiple courses at the same university, make absolutely sure that the two departments are separate, and are assessed by different admissions teams.

Some lucky applicants know exactly what they want to study and have selected the relevant Higher-Level subjects with this in mind. Their parents are in full agreement, and they have researched the most suitable universities appropriate for their academic potential and expectations. Others are not so lucky and remain undecided or torn between two or more interests which are not very compatible. This causes a big problem because it makes writing the personal statement an even more challenging task.

If the courses are related (like Business and Economics or Politics and History) it is quite well possible to write an appropriate personal statement. However, if the courses are less related (like Chemistry and Geography), it will be quite impressive if you manage to write a suitable personal statement that addresses both interests (and something we do not recommend!)

In these cases of diverse interests, it is advised to try to find some kind of combined courses that may be able to accommodate both of your passions. Alternatively, decide which subject you prefer more and structure your personal statement to that subject. An increasing trend at universities is to offer **dual interest courses** where you can decide which course to specialize in after the first year.

For example, UCL has introduced an Arts and Science course which allows you to decide which path to follow in your second year. You need to take a higher-level Arts/Humanities subject and a higher-level Science subject to be considered for this course. My alma mater, the New College of Humanities, also has similar options (see case study on NCH towards the end of this chapter).

There will be some applicants who feel obliged to study whatever it is their parents want them to do, rather than their own preference. It is often the case that they then end up being unhappy at university and also tend to struggle.

Pro Tip: It is **imperative that you absolutely know what you want to study** when applying. Changing course once you have started is difficult and should be avoided at all costs.

If you are deliberating several diverse subjects, you should try to find more general courses that will allow for specialization after the first year of university.

Those of you who know exactly what you want to study will have a much easier time applying - but it will still require lots of hard work and research. The first step should be to log onto UCAS and do an extensive course search. This will give you a rough idea of what is available out there, and you will get a feel for the range of possible degree paths.

For combined courses such as Politics *and* Philosophy, the 'and' implies a fairly equal distribution between the two subjects (you can usually choose to focus on one or the other in your second and third year).

In contrast, if the course is called Politics *with* Philosophy, this usually means that there will be a greater emphasis on Politics than on Philosophy. You can also delve deeper and check the specific outline of the course structure on the university's websites so you know exactly what the content split will be.

Pro Tip: Make sure that you read about the core and optional modules for your courses. The same course in two different universities can be wildly different and cover different topics (especially in the optional modules).

Courses with the exact same name will be different at each university, therefore you need to look at the course content and the optional subjects available. This information will be available on the course prospectus (the university should have the pdf document available) or just on the university website. You might also be interested in the ratio of exam results to coursework for your final grade. For example, if you know you perform stronger at essays and assessments, you should look for somewhere that places less emphasis on exams. Similarly, if you are an IB applicant who greatly enjoyed writing the Extended Essay, you might prefer an undergraduate course that involves writing a dissertation.[14]

[14] A dissertation is usually a 10,000-word essay which can be selected in place of an examined subject.

Pro Tip: Always look carefully at the **entry requirements** of your course choices. This means reading the fine print on websites, so you know **exactly** what is needed.

Nowadays, virtually all universities in the UK are well-versed in the IB Diploma and this is (finally and thankfully) reflected in the prospectus or website, which will list the typical IB requirements for the course.

You need to make sure you are able to meet any subject requirements. There is absolutely no point in applying to UCL to do Mechanical Engineering if you are not studying Mathematics and Physics at HL. Similarly, Medicine will normally require HL Chemistry and HL Biology.

These specific requirements will often differ slightly between universities, so you **need to check carefully**. If your subjects are appropriate, you still need to make a **realistic assessment** of your likelihood to get the grades needed.

Keep in mind that for the most competitive courses, the entry requirements constitute a *minimum* and that most successful applicants will have predicted grades much higher than what is stated. An optimistic prediction of 37 does not mean that you will receive an offer for a course that asks for 37. Courses that ask for 37 and above will be looking for academic potential at a higher level as well as an eye-catching profile (which is why the personal statement and references are oh-so-important). Many of these courses can fill their places several times over with applicants who have two or more points above their typical offer.

Pro Tip: You can actually check the ratio of applicants to places for most courses. This is a worthwhile exercise because it will show you just how competitive the UK university scene is.

As well as the overall requirements, you must consider any subject specific requirements for the course. If, for example, a course requires a 7 in HL Math and you have absolutely no chance in getting that 7, then you should not apply for that course.

You also need to check if there are any other requirements for the course. Some Law courses, for example, require that you take the LNAT exam, and some Medicine courses will require the UKCAT. Similarly, for social sciences and humanities, most Oxbridge colleges will require a good score of the TSA. These are subject-specific aptitude tests, and you are advised to visit the test website in order to do some practice questions to see how well you can perform. If it is obvious that you do not have an aptitude for these tests, you need to choose courses that do not require them.

Pro Tip: Make sure to have a range of grade boundaries (e.g., don't just have choices 35-36, have some under 35).

Choosing Your University

Once you have decided what to study, there are still several factors that might influence your choice of university or college. Obviously, you need to have a reasonable chance of getting in, you may want reassurance about the university's reputation, and its location will probably also be important to you. On top of that, most applicants have views about the type of institution they are looking for - big or small, old, or new, urban, or rural, specialist or comprehensive. You may surprise yourself by choosing somewhere that does not conform to your initial criteria but working through your preferences is another way of narrowing down your options.

One of the more obvious starting points when thinking about where to study is location. Most degrees in Scotland take four years, rather than the UK norm of three. Also, students normally pay little to no fees in Scotland, while those from the rest of the UK do. Nevertheless, Edinburgh and St Andrews remain particularly popular with international students.

Pro Tip: Start your university research **early** and be open to all kinds of options - don't be dead-set on one or just a couple of colleges.

A growing number of international students tend to look at the ease of traveling home from their university location. For those coming from Europe, London is a popular choice in this department because of the Eurostar services from King's Cross and the four main city airports - City, Heathrow, Gatwick, and Luton Stansted. You should get a rough idea of the travelling required to get home during the term breaks, or even if you wanted to go home for a long weekend.

The most popular universities in terms of total applications are usually all in the big cities - generally with other major centers of population within a two-hour travelling window. For those looking for the best nightclubs, sporting events, shopping, or a wide array of culture - in other words, most young people, and especially those who study in international schools close to city centers already - city universities are a magnet. The big universities, by definition, also offer the widest range of subjects, although that does not mean that they necessarily have the particular course that is right for you. Nor does it mean that you will actually use the array of nightlife and shopping that looks so alluring in the prospectus, either because you cannot afford to, because student life is too focused on the university, or even because you are too busy working.

Pro Tip: Ask yourself: am I a metropolitan city person? Or do I want to study in a small university town? Remember that you will be spending three years of your life there.

City universities are the right choice for many young people, but it is worth bearing in mind that the National Student Survey shows that the highest satisfaction levels tend to be at smaller universities, often those with their own self-contained campuses. It seems that students identify more closely with institutions where there is a close-knit community, and the social life is based around the students' union rather than the local nightclubs.

Few UK universities are in genuinely rural locations, but some - particularly among the newly promoted - are in relatively small towns. The only way to be certain of a university is to visit the university yourself (I know this has been impossible in recent times because of Covid). Schools often hold open days, and these should certainly not be ignored. The full calendar of events is available at www.opendays.com and on universities' own websites. Bear in mind, if you only attend one or two that the event has to be badly mismanaged for a university not to seem an exciting place to someone who spends his or her days at college. Try to get a flavor of several institutions before you make your choice.

Pro Tip: Almost all universities now have a dedicated YouTube channel and Instagram account. Definitely hop on and watch the videos where they interview current students and do a campus tour.

You must make sure that you are aware of the campus facilities provided and try to get some idea of student satisfaction by visiting social media sites where current students discuss their views regarding the university and the area.

Getting to know the university

As aforementioned, I would highly encourage you to try and visit the universities that interest you as most universities have several open days available. If you cannot make the official open days, most universities will agree to allow you to visit at some other time and might even be able to arrange for you to speak with someone about your chosen course.

The Oxford Study Courses (OSC) company runs a University Tour program which attracts IB students. They provide private tours of at least 12 different universities and colleges, as well as giving seminars and information sessions. Guidance and advice are available from experienced careers counsellors accompanying the tours and you get a chance to talk to admission officers and understand the differences in what each university offers. If you have the time and the finances available, I strongly recommend this tour - especially to those who know very little about UK universities in general.

Pro Tip: It is always best to visit universities **during term time** when there are students about so you can get a better feel for the atmosphere.

Again, I stress the importance of the resources at your disposal when it comes to choosing where to study - both free and paid. This book should only be your starting block when it comes to doing the necessary research. Our aim is to share with you what a typical IB student feels about their university and how well they fit in. By all means, please do consult the other big university guidebooks as they give a more detailed profile of universities (albeit from a UK-centric perspective), as well as providing rankings and other useful information.

Pro Tip: Checking rankings (e.g., the Times Good University Guide or Guardian guide.) can be a helpful activity to get a feel for things, but don't rely solely on rankings to make your choices.

Tips and Strategic Advice

If you send you application before the October 15th deadline and you are not applying for Medicine, it will be assumed (by universities that receive your application) that you have also applied to Oxford or Cambridge, despite the fact that your other choices are not directly visible to each university. Some applicants, who do not choose Oxbridge, think that by sending out an early application before the 15th of October, they can trick the prospective universities that they are also an Oxbridge applicant - and therefore, a better candidate.

Having spoken to many admission officers over the years, they are neither impressed nor tricked by this strategy and there is also a high likelihood that the strategy backfires. Although admissions officers do not openly admit it, there is some evidence to suggest that some highly competitive courses might reject applicants who they suspect have applied to Oxford or Cambridge (simply because they might feel they are 'wasting' giving an offer to that student if that student is Oxbridge bound). In my 15 years of helping IB students apply to the UK, I have known of several cases where a strong applicant got rejections in November from one or two of their other choices.

Pro Tip: Keep in mind that you DO NOT have to make all your choices at the same time. You can send your application with less than five choices and then add more at a later date.

This might actually be a workable strategy if you are unsure about some of your choices or if you want to 'test the water' to see what response you get from your initial choices. Some schools may even insist that you make all five choices at once. But remember, you are not obliged to do this (and in some cases, the schools are just misinformed...). You might only be interested in three or four courses, and you should feel comfortable leaving a choice open for later.

Here is my final advice with regards to the timing: do not send your application before the 15th of October unless you are actually applying to Oxbridge. At the same time, do not delay sending off your applications too late (end of October could be good, if you are ready then). This is particularly important if you are applying to extremely competitive courses. Most universities will look at applications as they come in. therefore, by sending your application in early, you do increase your chances of your application being considered quickly which will increase your chances of getting an early offer. If you get a decision before the winter break, then you focus more on your IB work.

If you send your application at the last minute, just before the January deadline, you might not hear back for a while from any of your choices. Moreover, there will be fewer spots available as some universities will have already given out some offers.

Nonetheless, there may actually be good reasons for delaying your application. For example, if you are undecided on your choices or if you are waiting for internal school results to improve, or if you have been too busy with your IA or EE deadlines. However, if there is no such reason, then it is advised to send your application as early as possible (but probably not before the Oxbridge deadline - unless you are applying there!)

Another little trick you can already use in the summer of your first year of IB involves looking at this year's Clearing information. In mid-august of the year that your application will be prepared, you have a golden opportunity to see which courses are oversubscribed and which might be less in demand or more flexible when results are published. Even though you will not be participating in that year's clearing, the clearing information available will give you a good insight into what you can expect for next year. If your first-choice course does not come out in clearing, then you can assume that it is highly competitive and will fill all its places with those holding the offer as a firm or insurance choice. This might mean, however, that the course selectors could possibly apply some flexibility at the results stage, being more willing to fill places with students holding an offer than to court new students through clearing. Unfortunately, for some universities it is a matter of pride that they do not offer courses in clearing.

If a course that interests you does come out in clearing and accepts a slightly lower grade, this suggests that there will be some flexibility at the results stage. Therefore, if you are predicted to meet the standard requirement you are likely to secure an offer. The longer a course remains in clearing, the greater the chances of getting an offer when you apply. By the same logic, a course that remains in clearing for a relatively long time suggests that it is undersubscribed and that you need not use one of your 5 choices to apply to it! What applies this year is highly likely (though not guaranteed) to apply next year. Therefore, you can confidently assume that the course will be available in clearing next year.

So how can you actually use this information to your advantage? Imagine you have the following replies from your choices:

Choice A: 36 points

Choice B: 35 points

Choice C: 26 points

Choice D / E: unsuccessful

Assuming that A, B, and C is the order of your preferences, you must face the dilemma of what to accept as your insurance. Conventional wisdom would suggest that you accept A as your firm and C as your insurance. If B is accepted as your insurance, you run the risk of not being accepted at either choice if you get 34 points or less. This is indeed the case, but if you end up with 35 points and are not accepted at your firm choice, you will be obliged to accept C and will miss out on B, which you prefer to C.

Here is where summer clearing information comes in handy. If your research has indicated that course C remained in clearing for more than two weeks and accepted applicants with 25 points (you can even try to find out this information through contacting students on internet forums devoted to IB, like reddit's r/ibo), it ceases to be too risky to accept A firmly and B as your insurance because the chances are that you will be able to get into C through clearing. Even if C is not available, a similar course is most likely to be available in clearing.

> **Pro Tip:** Each year's 'clearing' is a very good indicator of the relative difficulty of getting an offer or being accepted in the following academic year.

Your Schools University Counsellor

This is an extremely important individual - both for US and UK bound students. Plan a trip to their office sometime early in the first year - maybe even over the summer. Discuss your options and get as many resources as possible (they might have some great university application books in their office).

> **Pro Tip:** make sure to actually **consult your school's university counsellor** (even if they aren't that good). Normally they should be knowledgeable on a lot of these things.

The university counsellor should help you with all things related to college applications, but you would also be wise to do some research on your own (and check out my previous book on UK Universities - complete with student profiles)

Financing

UK tuition fees vary depending on your home country. For home students, English universities can charge up to a maximum of £9,250 per year for an undergraduate degree.

Institutions in Wales can charge up to £9,000 for home students and £3,925 for European Union and Northern Irish students. However, if you are Welsh student, you can apply for a fee grant to cover some of the cost of your tuition fees. This grant is currently not repayable, or income assessed.

Northern Irish universities will charge up to £4,275 for home students and may charge up to £9,250 for students from elsewhere in the UK.

Scotland does not charge home or EU students fees at undergraduate level, however, any student from England, Wales or Northern Ireland is expected to pay up to £9,250 per year. Non-EU international students will pay significantly more to study in Scotland.

In 2021, international students can expect to pay between £10,000 and £26,000 annually for lecture-based undergraduate degrees. An undergraduate medical degree can cost overseas students up to £58,600 per year. You can find your specific fees of courses that interest you on the university websites and prospectus. Please also try to take into account the cost of accommodation and living expenses when estimating total cost of studying in the UK (e.g., living in London is substantially more expensive than the rest of the UK).

With many universities charging the maximum fee, it is quite difficult to judge where you will get the best value for money and equally difficult to estimate this.

Pro Tip: The quality of teaching, hours of instruction per week, tutorial and small group provision and availability of bursaries and scholarships are super important to take into consideration.

In order to attract high caliber applicants, some universities offer financial assistance (through special offers of reduced fees or bursaries) to students who have high predicted grades hoping to induce applicants to commit to them as their firm choice. One Russell Group university actually converted conditional offers to unconditional if high scoring applicants made it their firm choice.

These inducements are likely to increase as universities want to attract high scoring applicants and you should research them carefully to take advantage of what is being offered. Several universities are making an effort to move up the ranking and this is assisted by increasing their average grade intake. Also, high scoring applicants help a university to improve its profile. The subsequent performance of these students, who are likely to secure good degrees, will further enhance the university's ranking.

Pro Tip: As a student, you will have several options on how to pay your fees and universities seem to be happy to make arrangements to suit you (you can either pay your fee in its totality for the year at the beginning or pay smaller amount across the year.)

Adjustment[15]

What is adjustment?

Adjustment is a process administered by the University and College Admissions Service (UCAS) and is used if you have *met and exceeded conditions for your firm choice.* Over 900 students successfully used adjustment in 2018 to change their university choice. Adjustment allows you to apply to universities that may not have accepted you with your predicted grades, asking if they will now accept you with your higher, actual grades. So, adjustment is a chance to *reconsider what and where to study.*

How does adjustment work?

Some applicants may have exceeded expectations, whilst others may have fallen just short, and others may have deferred their entry. This means that, in the transfer market that is university places, there could be spaces available on your favorite team (university)

[15] **Taken from EIB:** https://www.eibadmissions.com/resources/explaining-adjustment/

and in your favorite position (degree course). Excusing the analogy, this means that you could potentially switch to a different degree course at a different university that, at the time of making your application, you did not have the grades for. You can also reapply to universities that rejected your application previously, on the basis that you may be accepted with your higher grades.

When does adjustment open?

Adjustment opens from A-level results day until 31st August, but you will only have 5 days (including weekends) to accept a new offer. This time period starts from A-level results day or when your Conditional Firm (CF) offer becomes an Unconditional Firm (UF) offer on UCAS track (whichever occurs later). If this occurs after 26th August, you will only have until 31st August to apply through adjustment. The process is entirely optional, and some courses may remain full if all applicants have met their offers.

How can I adjust my university choice?

1. <u>Register on UCAS Track</u>

On A-level results day, you will have the option to register for adjustment in UCAS Track (which you should have used previously to track your application). If you accidentally sign up, please do not worry. As long as you do not apply to any other universities, the option for adjustment will disappear after 5 days and your current offer will remain safe.

2. <u>Considering different universities</u>

Unlike when you first applied, there is no list of universities offering adjustment places. Therefore, you will need to contact university admissions offices directly, asking whether they have any places available. To do this, you will need your UCAS personal ID so that they can check that you have exceeded your current offer. Once this is confirmed, you can then talk through the places they have available on their courses.

3. <u>Accepting an offer</u>

Once you have assessed which places are available, you can choose to accept one and only one offer. If you choose to stick with your current Unconditional Firm offer, you do not need to do anything, as the opportunity to adjust will disappear after 5 days and this choice will be confirmed. However, should you choose to accept an adjustment, you must let this university know so that they can add themselves to your application on UCAS track.

It is vitally important that you only accept one offer (verbally, over the phone, or via email) as this university will then add themselves as your chosen university on track. This university will then permanently replace your existing choice. This means that when you contact universities you are free to say you are just *researching* your options at this point, as this will allow you to talk with several universities without committing yourself to a place at any of them. Remember, you only get one offer through adjustment, so it is important that this choice is researched thoroughly!

Once you have accepted your offer, if you only applied to one course for the reduced £18 fee in January, you would have to pay the additional £6 to apply to more courses through adjustment. If you applied to more than one university earlier in the year, you should not need to pay anything extra. Once this process is complete, your track screen will update with your new university and course, and you will receive a letter from UCAS.

Top tips:

1. Do your research!

Do your research into student finance, available accommodation, campus life, the department and teaching style at the new institutions you are looking at – particularly as you may not have been to these universities before.

2. Visit the universities that you are interested in

Most universities have open days on the weekend after A-level results day. Ask other students who made it in through adjustment about their experiences and find out about your course structure, assessment, and module choices. Ask the universities about logistics – sorting out accommodation, student finance, bursaries. Get to know the university that you are considering adjusting to and its surrounding city or campus. Also, you should definitely talk to the university.

Having completed your research into how you reapply for student finance and accommodation, you will hopefully have communicated with the university about this process. Consider which university was the most responsive, as this will make the actual application process for these amenities easier.

3. Read up on other students' experiences of adjustment

You can find these by googling around or checking popular student forums.

4. Talk to the university about their offer

Remember to *agree an offer only verbally with a university if you are absolutely sure that you want it (UCAS).* Only one adjustment offer can be accepted and once it is accepted, even if this is over the phone, the university will change your offer on UCAS track, so please make sure you only accept an offer if you want the place. However, please do discuss your offer with the university to fully understand the course and university you are applying to and compare this with your current offer.

Remember, if you want to change courses at your existing university, you can call the university's admissions office to ask if you can change with your higher grades. Ask the university if this needs to be done through adjustment or can be completed once you arrive (although make sure it is clear how this will be done).

Should I participate in adjustment?

Adjustment is useful if you have exceeded expectations and want to go to a different university or study a different course. In addition, you do not have to accept any adjustment places that are offered to you, you can just say that you are researching at the moment (however, if you intend to accept one, remember the five-day window).

Having said this, it is always a good idea to be cautious when considering adjustment. Firstly, remember that you may be a little nervous about starting university - although it may look it, the grass is not always greener at a different university or studying a different course. Secondly, you have probably put a lot of work into researching your current university and course, so do not change your offer just because one university is ranked slightly higher than another.

If you do choose to change courses or universities, remember that you only get to accept one adjustment offer, and once it is agreed (via email or over the phone) you lose your current offer. This means it is all the more important to do thorough research into your options whilst you can. Research the syllabus, teaching style and accommodation of your new university, also considering the wider city or campus it is located in. Also, try and visit it if you can during their open day. Finally, consider the fact that you will have to reapply for accommodation, bursaries, and grants at your new university, which may take time away from enjoying your last month leading up to the big university departure.

Therefore, the key takeaway here is please don't feel pressured into using adjustment. If you want to change course with your higher grades, and this has been thoroughly researched, it may be a wonderful opportunity. But please do not feel ashamed in staying where you are. To finish, I would like to share with you one of the best pieces of advice I have come across, relating to adjustment, that was created by Flora Carr:

Imagine the prospect of swapping a very nice piece of chocolate cake (your existing offer) for a slightly bigger one (your adjustment place). If things don't work out quite as you'd hoped, it doesn't make the first slice any less sweet, does it?

Whichever piece of chocolate cake you choose, we hope that it is tasty, and we wish you the best of luck!

The Post-Brexit Situation

What does Brexit mean for students studying in the UK?

Even though negotiations between the UK and the EU have formally ended, it remains unclear what exactly will happen. Several scenarios are possible:

First and foremost, Brexit will likely not have any direct effect on students who would now and in the future be considered "international", i.e., from outside the EU/EEA.

It may be that the UK will agree to stay within the European single market; in that case, it is likely that European students would continue to be treated the same way as British students. Most importantly, that would mean that European students continue to pay only the lower tuition fees that also apply to British students. And for European students starting their studies in England in autumn 2022, the British government has confirmed that they will be treated like "home" students with regards to tuition fees and funding options.

In a "hard Brexit" scenario, it would be possible that European students would in the future be treated like non-European international students, meaning higher tuition fees.

Who is affected by Brexit?

As stated above, the immediate effects for international, non-European students are probably small.

If right now you would be classified as an "international student" by universities - as opposed to being a "domestic/EU student" - Brexit will likely not have an impact on your plans to study in the UK.

That means if you are from Asia, Africa or elsewhere outside the EU, you can relax. Your visa requirements as well as the level of the tuition fees you have to pay will be handled in the same way they are now.

However, if you are an EU citizen, you are currently treated the same way as UK students. That has previously meant fewer regulations and lower tuition fees. It is very likely that Brexit will change this comfortable situation for the worse. However, it is currently unclear just what exactly the effects will be.

Will tuition fees increase?

It is likely that Brexit will have some effect on tuition fees in the United Kingdom - but it is hard to predict what kind of clear effect.

Tuition fees charged from European students may increase if they are no longer treated like domestic British students. While the situation elsewhere in the UK is untransparent, Scotland has made very clear that, for its part, they plan to continue treating EU students the same as Scottish students, at least for any course started until autumn 2022.

The British economy and the strength of the British pound compared to other currencies also play a role. Within a year after the Brexit vote, the British pound lost around 15% of its value measured against the Euro (EUR). The economic turmoil brought about by a potential "Hard Brexit" is unforeseeable; it might be that the GBP would decline in value faster than universities can adjust their fees, making studies in the UK more affordable in the short term.

Is there a hostile atmosphere to international students in the UK?

There is no evidence that the British public are unhappy at the number of international students in the UK. Indeed, in a poll conducted in 2016, just 6 months after the Brexit vote, 75% of people who responded said they would like the number of international students in the UK to stay the same or rise. Further, it seems that of those who do wish to lower general immigration into the UK, only a small proportion count international students as immigrants. UK universities are also working hard to ensure they remain globally connected, welcoming places, and UK universities are certainly united in the aim of continuing to welcome students and researchers from around the world. Many of the UK's most well-respected institutions have shown support for the WeAreInternational campaign, including Oxford, Cambridge, the Russell Group, and UKCISA. The campaign hopes to "continue to ensure our research knows no geographical boundaries and our students and staff from around the world are able to celebrate their own cultures and friendships."

Will EU students need to apply for a student visa?

Controlling and limiting immigration has been at the heart of the public debate about Brexit. It is therefore possible that, in the wake of Brexit, new regulations will be introduced that will require students from the EU to explicitly apply for student visas to enroll at British universities. At the very least, it is likely that the Freedom of Movement for EU citizens will be limited.

Are international students no longer welcome in the UK?

Universities and educators have been very clear about this: International students are welcome in the UK. However, laws and visa policies are handled by the government; and the current administration has also publicly considered plans to limit immigration, including student immigration. There may be future policies making it harder for foreigners to study in the United Kingdom. That is why many students are now thinking about other countries in Europe that offer English-language degree programs, like Germany, Ireland, or the Netherlands.

Will the quality of teaching and research decline?

British universities enjoy a world-class reputation and regularly dominate international university rankings. If immigration into the UK should become harder for European academics, it is possible that talented European professors, teachers, and researchers would be forced to leave the UK or decide simply not to move to the UK. This might make it harder for universities to fill their academic positions with the most qualified candidates. At the same time, universities in the UK stand to lose billions of euros in research funding provided via the EU.

All of that might have an effect on the quality of teaching and research, but it is currently unclear to what extent the effects will be visible in the short or medium term.

What should you do if you want to study in the UK?

If you plan to enroll in a British university in the coming years, check their official website for their position on Brexit. It is likely there will be no discernable changes for those students who would have previously been classed as 'international' applicants (i.e., non-EU/EEA/CH), and we understand there are no major changes planned for the Tier 4 (student) visa, although of course we advise speaking with the British Council in your region for specific local advice. There is no set ratio between the number of students accepted paying 'home' rate fees and those paying international fees, so there should also be no shrinking of the places available to international students as the number of students eligible for home fee status shrinks.

UK University Profiles

Here is key information from **10 UK institutions that receive the most applications** from international IB students[16]:

KING'S COLLEGE LONDON

General admissions information[3]

King's welcomes students from the UK and across the globe studying the IB diploma. Offers will usually specify certain marks in three subjects at HL (usually in the ranges of 766–665), in addition to an overall point score of 35 for the whole diploma. The point score includes points for theory of knowledge and the extended essay. Admissions requirements vary for each programme.

Total undergraduate enrollment[4]	14k
Overall acceptance rate[5]	41%
Global ranking[6]	19
Average DP score[7]	37

Example course requirements

Business Management BSc: 35 points overall; three HL subjects at 766; at least one humanities or social science subject; plus mathematics and English language at GCSE grade B (or equivalent)

Additional considerations

http://www.kcl.ac.uk/study/ug/schoolscolleges/AdmissionsUpdates/revised-ib-offer.aspx

QUEEN MARY, UNIVERSITY OF LONDON

General admissions information

The IB diploma satisfies the entrance requirements for all degree programmes. Specific grades, subjects and levels are listed under the entry requirements for each course.

Total undergraduate enrollment	11k
Overall acceptance rate	59%
Global ranking	109
Average DP score	34

Example course requirements

Business Management BSc: 34 points overall; at least 6 in standard level (SL) English or 5 in HL English, and at least 4 in (any level of) mathematics

UNIVERSITY COLLEGE LONDON

General admissions information

The standard minimum requirement for IB diploma students is 34 points overall, with a combined score of 16 achieved in three HL subjects with no grade lower than 5. However, many programmes have higher entry requirements than this.

Total undergraduate enrollment	15k
Overall acceptance rate	44%
Global ranking	7
Average DP score	38

Example course requirements

Economics BSc: 39 points overall; a score of 19 points in three HL subjects including grade 7 in mathematics and grade 6 in economics if taken, with no score lower than 5

---

[16] From https://www.ibo.org/contentassets/5895a05412144fe890312bad52b17044/recognition---international-student-guide-uk--march2016---eng.pdf.pdf

UNIVERSITY OF BATH		
General admissions information		
The IB diploma is welcomed at Bath for all of our courses. Typical offers require an overall point score of 36 (including bonus points) alongside specified grades in three subjects at HL, ranging from 766 to 655 depending on course. Many courses require specific subjects to be studied at HL, although some of our courses will accept a required subject at SL as an alternative.	**Total undergraduate enrollment**	11k
	Overall acceptance rate	69%
	Global ranking	159
	Average DP score	36
Example course requirements		
Business Administration BSc (Hons): 36 points overall with 666 or 765 in three HL subjects.		
Additional considerations		
An IB diploma including English at SL or HL fulfils English language proficiency requirements.		

UNIVERSITY OF EDINBURGH		
General admissions information		
Admissions requirements vary for each programme. IB diploma candidates are required to obtain the award of the diploma at a specific overall grade and to have achieved specific grades in three HL subjects.	**Total undergraduate enrollment**	18k
	Overall acceptance rate	37%
	Global ranking	21
	Average DP score	36
Example course requirements		
Business and Economics MA: Award of diploma with 34 points overall and grades 655 in HL subjects including mathematics; SL: mathematics at 6 (if not taken at HL) and English at 4		
Additional considerations		
Unless a HL is specified in the stated entry requirements, a score of at least 4 is required in IB English SL.		

UNIVERSITY OF EXETER		
General admissions information		
The university recognizes the IB and its programme listings give full details of the grades and subjects required. Offers are usually based on the overall IB diploma grade but could also include achieving specific grades in specific subjects. IB diploma students must receive their diploma, as well as at least two HL subjects with a score of 4 or higher.	**Total undergraduate enrollment**	15k
	Overall acceptance rate	80%
	Global ranking	161
	Average DP score	35
Example course requirements		
Economics BSc: 34–38 points overall		
Additional considerations		
SL grade 5 or HL grade 4 or above fulfills English language proficiency requirements.		

UNIVERSITY OF WARWICK		
General admissions information		
The university is committed to giving full and fair consideration to all entry qualification information presented by individual applicants. We welcome applications from candidates offering many different qualifications, including the International Baccalaureate. Typical offers are listed under each course entry, and you should check the listed entry requirements for the course you are interested in.	**Total undergraduate enrollment**	13k
	Overall acceptance rate	63%
	Global ranking	48
	Average DP score	37
Example course requirements		
International Management BSc. (Hons): 38 points overall		

UNIVERSITY OF ST ANDREWS		
General admissions information		
IB candidates are expected to obtain scores ranging from 35 to 38 points. Individual courses have their own entry requirements.	**Total undergraduate enrollment**	7k
	Overall acceptance rate	39%
	Global ranking	68
	Average DP score	36
Example course requirements		
Economics BSc (Hons): 38 points overall		
Additional considerations		
IB scores are considered as satisfying English language requirements. English A: Literature or language and literature—SL 4/5 or HL 5/6 depending on course; English B—SL 6/7 or HL 4/5 depending on course; history—SL 4/5 or HL 4/5 depending on course.		

UNIVERSITY OF KENT		
General admissions information		
The university welcomes applications from students offering the full IB diploma. Offers are made solely on the basis of the IB marking scheme and not the UCAS tariff. There is a standard IB diploma offer of 34 points across all programmes including any specific subjects at HL or SL required by the particular degree programme. As an alternative to achieving 34 points, for most programmes, the university will also make IB students the offer of passing the IB diploma with specific achievement in HL/SL subjects.	**Total undergraduate enrollment**	15k
	Overall acceptance rate	82%
	Global ranking	360
	Average DP score	32
Example course requirements		
Business Administration BBA (Hons): 34 points overall, or 16 at HL including mathematics 4 at HL or SL		
Additional considerations		
Students offering a combination of IB certificates and other qualifications, such as the IB Career-related Programme, will also be considered on their individual merits and should contact the Recruitment and Admissions Office for additional guidance.		

UNIVERSITY OF MANCHESTER		
General admissions information		
If students have completed a full IB diploma, they can be considered for direct entry to undergraduate courses. The university's minimum entry criteria for the IB range from 32 to 37 points depending on individual course requirements, with a normal expectation of grade 6 or 7 in relevant HL subjects. Some schools stipulate specific grades and subjects at HL, as well as a minimum number of overall points.	**Total undergraduate enrollment**	26k
	Overall acceptance rate	62%
	Global ranking	33
	Average DP score	35
Example course requirements		
Accounting BSc: 37 points overall; 666 in HL subjects, plus no less than 5 for SL English and 6 for mathematics (mathematical studies not accepted)		
Additional considerations		
SL 5 of the IB diploma satisfies the university's minimum English language requirement.		

Most Popular UK Universities for Overseas Students

Overseas students are not a rarity in the UK. These are the top 15 universities with the highest proportion of international undergraduates and postgraduates in the UK:

1. University College London: 12,742
2. The University of Manchester: 10,880
3. The University of Edinburgh: 8,138
4. Coventry University: 7,658
5. The University of Sheffield: 7,486
6. King's College London: 7,054
7. The University of Liverpool: 6,919
8. University of the Arts, London: 6,689
9. The University of Leeds: 6,566
10. The University of Birmingham: 6,498
11. The University of Warwick: 6,440
12. Imperial College of Science, Technology and Medicine: 6,277
13. University of Nottingham: 5,896
14. London School of Economics and Political Science: 5,776
15. The University of Glasgow: 5,510

CHAPTER 5

THE UK ADMISSION PROCESSES

In this chapter we will present the views of actual university staff who are involved in the applications and selection processes. A representative sample of universities has been selected, mainly from the Russell Group, beginning with five that are part of the University of London, and which constitute very popular choices for IB students.

The introduction of up to £9000 fees has influenced the selection and admissions practices of some universities and has intensified competition to attract the best applicants. Fortunately, IB applicants are generally regarded to be strong, and some universities have revised their IB offers downwards, while others have introduced new scholarships and bursaries to attract applicants with high IB scores.

Of particular interest is the recent decision by King's College London to reduce all of its IB offers to 35 points overall, while placing greater emphasis on higher level subject scores. e.g., 7,6,6 for the most competitive courses and 6,6,5 for the less competitive courses. The equivalent A-Level grades are respectively A*, A, A and A, A, B.

According to Paul Teulon, Director of Admissions: 'King's is committed to a clear, fair and transparent admissions policy and want to ensure that candidates are considered appropriately and holistically. In the development of our new range of IB offers, we have sought to reduce the potential unfairness which we feel may have inadvertently crept into IB offers in recent years. We are seeking to ensure that IB students, like students following other curricula, with the qualities to excel at King's are made appropriate offers.'

The prospectus goes on to say: "King's has noted that despite the average IB student's grades remaining relatively constant throughout the past decade, for a variety of reasons the admissions requirements have increased. Our new range of admissions requirements seeks to redress this balance and ensure that IB students, like students following other curricula, with the qualities which will allow them to excel at King's are made appropriate offers."

Oliver Selwood who is the Undergraduate Admissions Manager for Arts and Sciences at King's College further confirmed this IB friendly attitude. Despite being extremely busy, he agreed to be interviewed and happily answered my questions about King's selection process and the suitability of IB applicants.

The following is a summary of his views and responses:

1. IB is the second most popular source of applicants, estimated to be about 20% of the total.
2. Many courses are oversubscribed, so late entries are not usually accepted except in a few subjects.
3. Admissions staff process applications and only marginal cases are referred to academic tutors.

4. IB is considered to be rigorous and desirable for its wide range of subjects.

5. The Extended Essay is important for some courses, as is the choice of subjects.

6. Interviews are rare for Arts and Sciences courses, although courses in the Health Schools such as Medicine and Nursing interview as a matter of course.

7. From the personal statement a sense of commitment is desired and references to the course are useful for showing preferences. Work placements are potentially useful and extracurricular activities are sometimes considered, but overall, it is the desire to study a particular subject at King's that needs to be seen.

8. The reference should confirm the academic ability and potential of the applicant and provide any important supplementary information which is relevant, especially to justify a high prediction for an applicant with a weak background. It is also important in flagging up any mitigating circumstances to be considered. Overall, it is felt that it is rare to read a bad reference, although this is one of the criteria used to make decisions on applications.

9. The truthfulness of the statement and the reference, and the extent to which the statement is the work of the applicant is an important consideration and all necessary plagiarism checks are carried out. Admissions departments used software to do this, and it is also flagged up by UCAS.

10. Since most courses are oversubscribed, very few clearing places are ever available and similarly very few adjustment places are accepted.

I questioned the new policy of giving all successful IB applicants a standard offer of 35 points and suggested that this policy runs the risk of encouraging applicants with a weaker academic profile, resulting in even more applicants for already oversubscribed courses. I gave the example of Business Management, which, in my opinion, would attract many more applications now that the offer has been reduced from 38 points and as a result the decisions about offers would be significantly delayed. (His opinion was that the retention of high grades for the HL subjects should minimize this risk.)

Pro Tip: Apply to the university of your dreams and don't sell yourself short. You never know...

The London School of Economics and Political Sciences is a very popular choice for IB applicants, and for many the question of how to get an offer is one of life's great mysteries. The prospectus is very detailed with considerable information on the admissions criteria and the personal statement, but getting an offer remains a great challenge. Academic ability and potential is very important, but there is no shortage of IB applicants with 42+ predictions who are unsuccessful for courses that require 37 or 38 overall. Very often it will be the choice of subjects that is at fault. You should, therefore, consult the website which provides a list of preferred subjects. For many courses, a 7 in HL Mathematics is required and it is advisable to include some indication of mathematical ability and application in addition to the prediction of a 7.

I was able to gain a more detailed insight into the whole process from an interview with Linda Hamer who is an Access & Admissions Specialist at LSE. She explained that a system of filters is applied and that applications are examined as they arrive.

1. The first filter is performed by admissions staff who carefully consider the evidence of academic and subject specific ability. If this is seen to be inadequate, the application will be filtered out, unless the reference addresses the problem satisfactorily.

2. The second filter is holistic and looks at all the sections of the application. Experienced admissions selectors are involved in this filter, and it is here that the personal statement will be scrutinized, in addition to the academic profile. The selectors are very skilled in spotting over-estimation of academic ability and can confidently distinguish between genuine personal statements and those with too much outside help. Above all, the statement has to convey a genuine academic interest in the subject and display suitability for studying at the LSE. The Extended Essay is potentially useful. It is also advisable to provide evidence of knowledge and interest that goes beyond the syllabus in the key subjects. Appropriate knowledge of contemporary issues is desirable.

University College London is another popular destination for IB students, offering a wide spectrum of courses all of which are highly competitive. In addition to informal chats with admissions staff, I was able to have two interviews with academic tutors who take a very direct interest in the selection of candidates for their respective courses. The first interview was with Stephen Todd, who is Program Director, BSc/MSci Management Science and Senior Teaching Fellow, Management Science, and Innovation.

Management Science is a relatively new degree course, with its first intake in 2014, and is looking for applicants with good mathematical skills, entrepreneurial drive and strong leadership qualities who can work well in teams. It is interdisciplinary, combining engineering principles with quantitative mathematics, economics, and finance. The course attracted 735 applicants and about 180 of these will be made an offer anticipating an intake of around 100. IB applicants are considered to be highly suitable, and the standard offer this year was **38** points with **6, 6, 6** at Higher Level, to include Mathematics. The Extended Essay is also recognized to be a useful preparation. As there is no shortage of highly qualified applicants, the personal statement is heavily relied on to identify suitable candidates. In addition, the applicants with the most potential will be sent a questionnaire to fill in, which has a variety of questions aiming to gauge the 'raw potential' that the selector is looking for.

Ideally, a mix of 50% UK/EU and 50% International is hoped for. The successful applicant will be able to work well in a team, sometimes leading and sometimes following. Qualities of entrepreneurship are important, and the course encourages intensive analysis of innovation. The questionnaire attempts to identify these qualities.

The course is quickly developing links with foreign universities and with prospective employers reflecting its practical nature and variety. The course regards itself as a peer to Stanford and MIT. Furthermore, it aims to fill a perceived gap in the market for practical or vocational management learning.

The second interview was with Richard Pettinger who is Principal Teaching Fellow in Management Education | Course Director, BSc/MSci Information Management for Business | Management Science & Innovation. A summary of his views is presented here:

- **On the IB:** It is very varied - more so than A-levels, and so we are very happy to consider people from this background; it is an excellent grounding for University study (whether students come to do our program or any other); we have a requirement of 36 as you know, which UCL equates to AAB at A-level.

- **Personal statements:** my advice always is - do it yourself! Don't go to a consultant or anything like that - statements that are prepared by others stand out a mile; structure and organize it so that the student says: why they want to go to a particular university (if it is one that has perceived high standing like ours then nod a bit in the direction of what is offered there); what they expect to get out of the course; what they are going to contribute to the course and the university; what else they would like to get from their university stay; and any particular achievements that they have had to date.

- **Interviews:** we no longer use them, though we will always meet with people either here or on their own territory (and our international office sends people all over the world to meet with prospective students).

- **Final decision:** a combination of all of the above; we make offers based on the whole application. Predicted final grades obviously help - but if someone was predicted low grades but the rest of their application 'stacked up' then we would make an offer. Similarly, if the predicted grades are very high but the rest of the application is poor then we would turn it down. So, it all has to be right.

- **General appreciation of the IB:** we are all happy with it - it is universally recognized across UCL, and we all look at applications with IB exactly as we look at A-levels.

Although not a member of the Russell Group, the **School of Oriental and African Studies (SOAS)** is a highly respected and competitive member of the University of London. As well as a wide range of language-based courses, SOAS also offers courses in Economics, Law, and International Politics. For Economics, the standard offer is 38 points overall with 7, 6, 6 at higher level, which is the same as LSE and UCL.

I was able to interview Nick Butler, who is the Head of Admissions, and he began by stating that SOAS is very IB-friendly, valuing both the subject spread and the requirement of a second language:

- The selection process is centralized and as applications are received, they are appraised according to a set of criteria, the most important being academic achievement and potential, as indicated by actual and predicted grades. If an applicant's academic profile is satisfactory, an offer will be made.
- In marginal cases the personal statement will also be reviewed, and the application will be passed on to the relevant department for a final decision.

Mr. Butler was the first admissions officer to openly admit that the personal statement was not of paramount importance but mainly used to choose among marginal cases. The assumption was that SOAS attracts applicants who have a particular interest in 'development' issues related to their chosen subjects and so a further interest or commitment as expressed in a personal statement is not necessary.

What is essential is a strong academic background and evidence of the ability to do well on a rigorous and challenging undergraduate degree course. Some courses, such as Economics, Law, Politics, and International Relations, are usually oversubscribed. However, admissions staff are very experienced and are able to identify those who are likely to do well and those who deserve an offer.

Unlike some other members of the University of London, SOAS is not reluctant to offer courses through clearing and is also happy to accept students through adjustment. The fact that the standard offer for the most competitive courses is quite high, should discourage frivolous applications and attract only those who are aware of the rather special nature of the degrees. The philosophy at SOAS is : 'if you have the grades, we are happy to have you'.

Queen Mary College is a relatively new member of the Russell Group and has recently been creeping up the rankings in many subject areas such as Law and Medicine. Marlon Gomes, the Head of Admissions, is a very experienced and well-informed selector who has an excellent knowledge of the IB and its equivalence to other qualifications.

- A steady increase in applications has meant some slightly higher offers. However, the aim is to keep the offers unchanged, as far as possible, in order to encourage applicants from state schools and from the local area.

- The typical offer for Law is still 36 points despite being very oversubscribed as a result of its top 5 ranking and this makes the selection process much more difficult.

- The selection process takes the form of recommendations by the admissions staff and course selectors make the final decisions.

- The admissions staff are generally trusted to identify those applicants with the correct academic profile and the course selectors will only need to decide on marginal cases.

- The policy is to view applications as they come in and Queen Mary is usually one of the first universities to reply to applicants.

- Furthermore, highly qualified applicants are offered attractive scholarships if they make Queen Mary their firm choice.

- The admissions philosophy is that the academic profile is the most important criterion, and much weight is given to the predicted grades. In light of this, Mr. Gomes would prefer a post-results admissions process to the current pre-results offer system.

- In addition, he would support the introduction of extra tests by the Russell Group as a further source of information about academic ability and potential. Nevertheless, he is happy that the current system works well and that applicants to Queen Mary are dealt with fairly and efficiently.

- In view of the possible lack of transparency, the personal statement is seen as a potential landmine that often detracts from, rather than enhances, an application. Some courses conduct interviews for shortlisted applicants, but most courses are not able to do this, except for special cases.

- Medicine is quite separate from the general applications process and is handled exclusively by the department. Interviews are always required before an offer is made.

All of the London Universities reviewed above are part of the UCAS process. However, there is another university in London that is independent of UCAS. It is the **New College of the Humanities (NCH)**. Its founder and Master, Professor

Anthony Grayling, is adamant that exam results are an insufficient indicator of academic suitability, and that supplementary evidence is needed. In a written statement he presented the following views:

- "I am skeptical about the value of examinations, and even more skeptical about the validity of judging anyone's ability only on the basis of the numbers or letters on a piece of paper.

- Being an admissions tutor in higher education is a good basis for assessing how reliable exam results are as a measure of a person's true abilities.

- Because of the large numbers of students applying for university every year, most universities look at the paperwork only, and rely on grades as the final determiner.

- But if you interview candidates, read longer pieces of work they have produced during their studies, look at their curricula vitae and their references from their schools, a fuller and much more accurate picture emerges.

- On that basis, a thoughtful institution can back its own judgment about the capacity of a candidate to mature and develop as a mind and a person, which is what the aim of higher education should be.

- The process just described is time-consuming and labor-intensive. That means it is expensive. For these reasons very few institutions do it.

- The result is a crude system of selection massively over-reliant on grades, made worse by the fact that the exam system, which awards those grades, is so deeply imperfect.

- In an ideal world there would be few examinations, and their use would be confined to getting students to sum up and bring together the fruits of their studies. At most the resultant grades would be indicative.

- Only the reading of longer pieces of work which have been more carefully prepared, and interviews, can really reveal genuine capacities and abilities; and these should be the basis of selecting students for higher study.

After frequent discussions I have had with Jane Phelps, the Director of External Relations, and other admissions staff at the **New College of the Humanities**, I can confirm that they are extremely IB friendly and have a high regard for IB applicants who are considered to be especially well suited to the structure of NCH courses.

- The standard offer is 36 points with 6, 6, 6 at Higher Level. For some courses specific subjects are preferred; for example, Economics requires Mathematics at Higher Level. However, applicants with Standard Level Mathematics will also be considered and if accepted, are invited to attend a Math preparation course during the summer to ensure an appropriate level of competence in the mathematical skills required for the course.

- Part of the applications procedure involves the submission of a piece of work relevant to the subject. For this, the Extended Essay, or at least a draft of the Essay, is judged to be suitable because it shows the ability to develop analysis in an extended example of written work, as described by Professor Grayling.

- If the academic profile is good and the personal statement shows the necessary commitment and interest, the applicant will be invited to attend an interview. In certain circumstances, the interview might be conducted via Skype, but the preference is for the interview to take place at NCH so that the applicant is able to have a tour of the University and experience the atmosphere of the place.

The rest of the chapter will examine admissions practices at some UK universities outside London.

Gareth Carey-Jones was able to give me a good indication of how **Exeter University** considers IB applicants. His views are summarized as follows:

- In common with most other UK universities, we make offers to IB applicants in terms of total points as that is currently the way entry requirements for IB applicants are best understood. We have considered and will continue to consider moving to making offers differently, asking for grades in three Higher level subjects rather than an overall IB points score.

- The typical range of offers is 38 points for courses requiring A*A A to 34 points for courses requiring A A B.

- We work as a partnership. Criteria are agreed with academic tutors ahead of each application cycle. Those criteria are then used by admissions staff to make decisions. With respect to the personal statement, he referred me to the website which states: "The most important aspect of your application will be your achieved or predicted academic results, as this is the best predictor for success on one of our degree programs.

- Personal statements will be considered, but mainly to identify any mitigating or extenuating circumstances that may have affected your achieved or predicted grades.

Where personal statements are considered more closely, we would want to see:

1. Your reasons for the choice of subjects taken in IB and, where appropriate, the relevance of those subjects to your chosen degree course.

2. Why you have applied for a particular course and how this relates to your current and previous studies and experiences. If you have a career goal, it is helpful if you tell us how the course would enable you to fulfil that ambition.

3. Evidence of a willingness and desire to learn at a higher level: we are looking for students who have the potential and the drive to succeed.

4. Details of any work experience, paid or unpaid, and any other positions of responsibility that you've had. We're particularly interested in the skills gained from these experiences and how they relate to your own personal development and how they may help you in your studies and life at university.

5. Information regarding volunteering and other extracurricular activities and what you have gained in terms of experience and skills from these interests. Finally, adjustment is accepted depending on places and extra tests for non-medical course are not used.

York is another popular Russell Group university and Lee Hennessy - Deputy Head of Recruitment & Admissions was able to provide the following answers to some questions:

Q1. How do you view IB applicants?

Very positively.

Q2. Is the main selection process conducted by admissions staff or by academic tutors?

Central admissions staff.

Q3. How important is the personal statement?

The weighting given to the personal statement depends on the program but every PS is read twice and forms part of our holistic assessment of the application. The difficulty is that we can never be sure whether it is wholly the candidate's work. We have to assume that it is and in some cases a strong personal statement will make all the difference between receiving or not receiving an offer.

Q4. Do you accept applicants through adjustment?

Very few.

Q5. Would you like to see more external tests such as LNAT?

The only external test we ask for is STEP for our mathematics programs.

Birmingham University is looking to attract top students by converting conditional offers into unconditional for applicants with high grades or predicted grades who make the university their first choice. Joanna Labudek, the Head of Admissions, confirmed that:

- IB applicants are treated in the same way as A - Level applicants and that the unconditional offer practice was extended to IB applicants as well . She went on to say : " We consider the qualification to be robust and believe that it prepares students for higher education . "

- With respect to the main selection process , academic tutors set all entry criteria but for some programs this is applied in practice by admissions staff on the applications we receive .

- The personal statement is important , for competitive programs it is very important in determining whether an offer will be made , for less competitive programs it can still make the difference between being accepted or declined if an applicant is borderline .

- Applicants through adjustment are accepted and external tests are not deemed necessary .

All of the above comments from admissions staff are quite typical and represent the general attitude to IB applicants which is invariably positive. It would be repetitive to include more universities with regard to general admissions practices for academic courses as the views of admissions officers are very similar with respect to IB applicants.

I will, however, include a final report from one of the leading universities for Drama in the UK , the **Central School of Speech and Drama (CSSD)** .

Ollie Mawdsley, the Admissions Officer, provided the following answers to my questions:

Q1. Is the IB held in high regard or are applications from IB candidates less competitive than A - Level students?

IB candidates are held in no higher nor lower esteem than A - Level or BTEC candidates . We aim to give all candidates the same opportunities , as we are aware that success in our degrees is just as likely to be as a result of talent and hard work as it is of academic background.

Q2. Are applicants interviewed for all undergraduate courses?

Yes, everyone is interviewed, as we believe this gives people the best possible opportunity to show us what they have to offer.

Q3. In your experience, who usually helps students prepare for their auditions?

I assume you're talking about the BA (Hons) Acting auditions . Most of our applicants for this course are involved in a drama group of some sort , either as part of their school life or as an extracurricular activity , and in our experience , the people who run these groups are often more than happy to give up their time in order to help someone with the drive and talent to audition for drama school . For our other two BA courses , it's normally the drama or art teachers at school who help the applicants with their interview prep .

Q4. Do admissions officers or academic tutors conduct the main selection process?

For all of our courses , the interviews and auditions are conducted by academic tutors at Central , both permanent and visiting staff members who have worked extensively on the courses here .

Q5. How important is the personal statement and how much does it influence the selection decision ?

The personal statement is important to us as a means of furthering discussion regarding the applicant's experience, interests, and ideas. Due to our fairly intensive interview procedures, those with poor personal statements still have a chance to show us what matters to them; however, it makes the process much easier all round if people are honest and passionate with their statements.

Pro Tip: do NOT be let down if your dream university does not accept you. There are so many different factors which are outside of your control that determine if you get an offer or not.

Additional Resources

Books:

For interviews with IB students at over 50+ UK universities, we suggest the following book:

- **The Good University Guide for IB Students [UK 2019 Edition]** by Alexander Zouev, 2019

Websites:

You can find out more about each university's attitudes towards the IB and their application process by emailing the admissions office of your chosen university.

CHAPTER 6

OXBRIDGE

Most admissions staff and tutors acknowledge that one of the best methods of selecting suitable applicants is with an interview. In practice, logistics involved in conducting comprehensive interviews tend to prohibit their use and most universities and courses do not normally invite applicants for an interview. There are, however, some notable exceptions where the interview is deemed to be the decisive element in the selection process.

Pro Tip: Both Oxford and Cambridge hold interviews for all their courses and state clearly that no applicant will receive an offer without having been interviewed.

Similarly, for medicine (which we cover in the next chapter) you are most likely going to be interviewed. The interview is the final stage of the application process, and you will only reach this stage if your application is considered good enough and if you appear to satisfy the other admissions criteria. Only a certain portion of applicants are called for an interview, and you should not assume that getting an interview is a given, or that an interview indicates you will be admitted.

Application Process

As noted in the previous chapter, the application deadline for Oxbridge is in mid-October, and applications are accepted from September until this date. Both Oxford and Cambridge are collegiate universities, which means that you will not only apply to the university, but to a specific college of the university. You do not necessarily have to specify your college of choice when you apply and you can do this by making an 'open application', but you will be allocated to a specific college if accepted.

Pro Tip: Many applicants will have a preferred college, but you must ensure that the college you select actually teaches the subject you wish to apply for!

You can find this by reading the university prospectus or consulting the college website. Those who do not have a preferred college may consult the listing of relative competitiveness of the various colleges for different subjects. Unofficially, some colleges are considered more prestigious for certain subjects than others. Nevertheless, you should not automatically avoid the most competitive college for a given course, because it might be the case that the majority of applicants do this and as a result the more competitive colleges have fewer applicants.

Pro Tip: Somewhat anecdotal, but from the successful Oxbridge applicants we have tutored, most of them did an 'open application' (did not specify which college). The sample size here is too small to be significant, but we do recommend you consider this instead of applying to the 'famous' colleges.

Once your application has been received, it will be considered, initially, as with any other university, **on the basis of actual and predicted grades.** Applicants for these universities and courses will only be encouraged by their schools if they are strong enough, so it is expected that most applications are potentially good enough to secure an offer. The next step will normally be for some additional evidence of suitability to be exhibited.

This could take the form of supplementary tests for Oxbridge such as the Thinking Skills Assessment (TSA) and in the case of medical subjects, the UK Clinical Aptitude Test (UKCAT) or the Biomedical Admissions Test (BMAT). In addition, some Oxbridge colleges might ask for an example of written work to be sent to them.

Together with the information on your application form, these additional test results will be considered in order to decide whether you are a strong enough candidate to be called for interview. Note that not all courses require additional tests. If your chosen course does have such a test requirement, you are strongly advised to consult the test web sites and do some of the practice tests that are available. The more practice you do, the better your final performance will be.

If, after these initial stages, you are called for an interview, it means that you are deemed to be a strong applicant who is potentially worthy of a place. The interview will now be the final hurdle, after which the suitable applicants will be made an offer.

Oxbridge Interviews

As with many aspects of the application process, there is a wonderful mythology that has evolved around the Oxbridge interviews. If some of the stories were true it would put the trauma experienced during the interview on par with the most painful of childhood experiences.

It is generally acknowledged that stories such as that one kid setting fire to the tutor's newspaper in response to the request: 'Do something to surprise me' are urban myths. Similarly, you will not have a rugby ball thrown at you to test your athletic ability. Entertaining as these stories are, they bear no resemblance to the typical Oxbridge interview.

The aim of the interview is to confirm the academic potential that you appear to possess. All of the applicants who are called for interview are potentially suitable candidates for an offer of a place and are quite similar with respect to their academic profile (of course there are some students who are simply prodigies/wonderkids). The interview is your chance to show that you are suitable for the course and also provides you with the opportunity to decide whether the course is appropriate for you and whether you will feel comfortable spending the next three years in this type of environment.

Nearly all of the Oxbridge admissions tutors that I have spoken to were adamant that their aim is not to scare the applicant with impossibly hard question or expose their lack of knowledge, but rather to give the interviewees the opportunity to display their ability to think and question. They want to see how you do under pressure, and they want a glimpse of your thought process and critical thinking skills.

Pro Tip: They are not concerned to see if you know the correct answers, but rather in your ability to examine and consider situations that you are not familiar with.

They want to test your academic potential by observing how you go about trying to work out an answer to question, as opposed to merely testing whether you know the answer. To do this, they will ask you to consider theoretical situations or abstract problems in order to judge your deductive capabilities and your thought processes. Sometimes, you will be given something to read before the interview and you will then be asked about your interpretation or understanding of some of the points that were detailed in the extract.

Applicants for **Literature** might be given a poem to read and then will be asked to discuss some aspects of it with the view to recognizing the applicant's ability in determining the meaning of the poem and the use of historical or other references.

Applicants for **Social Sciences** might be given an extract about the environment or a proposed government policy to read so that a discussion of the important issues can be pursued in the interview. Again, the aim is to see if you can present your arguments and views in a coherent and convincing manner, having considered the question from different angles. There is no right or wrong. However, there are various implications and parameters that could be identified and it is this skill that you are being tested on.

If you are a Math and Science applicant, you might be given a problem to solve as a test of your ability, but again you will not be judged exclusively on whether or not you find the correct answer. The aim is to see how you go about trying to find the answer, in order to see how you apply your scientific or mathematical knowledge.

It should be clear by now that the aim of the interview is not to make you squirm because you do not know the answer to an impossibly difficult question. On the contrary, it can give you the opportunity of showing how you go about trying to find an answer, how you react to an unfamiliar situation and how you apply lateral thinking in order to try to deduce something meaningful. This is what they want to see in order to gauge your potential and ability to think beyond the facts.

Whilst waiting at the college for your interview to occur, you may have the opportunity to ask other applicants who have already had their interview what kind of questions were asked. I would proceed here with great caution. First, it is in the best interest of the other applicants to not assist you (because they are competing for the same spot). Therefore, there is a good chance they will throw you off or simply lie. Second, even if you did find out exactly what the tutors will ask you - it will be pretty evident to them that you have found out beforehand. These are seasoned Oxbridge academics, they will be able to tell if you have specifically prepared an answer for a specific question, no matter how good your acting is. If you simply regurgitate a prepared answer to a question you knew was coming, they don't actually get to see what they want to see - which is how your brain works when facing something new!

Pro Tip: If you have the opportunity to find out what kind of questions will be asked, proceed with caution. While it's great to know an answer, but you still want to show some live thinking skills.

A typical interview will be conducted by two academics familiar with the course you are applying for. There will, normally, be a second interview with two different academics and you might also be asked to stay around for an interview at another college (this is called getting 'pulled'). You will be given the option of staying at the college overnight, but you can travel to the college on the day of the interview. You should, of course, make sure that you arrive early enough to avoid unnecessary anxiety.

Staying at the college is recommended because it gives you a taste of college life and helps you to imbibe the atmosphere of the place. You might also meet other students with whom you can share your anxieties and impressions.

The Interview Process

1. At the start of your interview you will be asked a neutral question to relax you and break the ice. Then, there will be a sequence of questions that will give you the opportunity of expressing yourself on familiar ground. This could involve some questions relating to points you have mentioned in your personal statement and, possibly, a brief discussion of your Extended Essay topic. It is

essential that you are familiar with your personal statement and that you have actually read the books or articles that you claim to have impressed you.

Pro Tip: make sure you know your personal statement well enough for interviews. I know everyone says this, but seriously - make sure you know it (e.g., results of IAs/experiments, your personal reflection on an activity). They may not ask you about it, but it's worth it for the security of knowing there's a few questions you can answer comprehensively!

2. Very quickly, the discussion will be directed to some issues relevant to your course with the aim of hearing your opinion and how you arrived at it. You might be asked about some current development in your subject, and you should try to be up to date with such developments and with current affairs in general. You are expected to have some social and political awareness and to be able to discuss ethical issues with a degree of confidence and conviction. Some questions might aim to test your knowledge, but most will be aimed at testing your powers of analysis and clarity of thought and expression. Your opinion about an actual or hypothetical event might be sought and you should not rush to respond but should take a minute or two to actually think about your answer (I sometimes even say in the interview, out loud, 'I'm just going to take a second to think this out.'). Do not be scared to ask for clarification if you have not fully understood the question (and this can also buy you some more thinking time if you strategize it well).

3. At the end of the interview, you will probably be asked if you have any questions. You should take this opportunity to confirm your interest in the course and college by asking a pertinent question. This could relate to one of the optional courses that is

offered, the structure of teaching or whether an interest of yours is catered for

Pro Tip: Have a question or two pre-planned, but if something comes up in the interview that you want to ask at the end about - do that! You can even say 'I had a question prepared, but this bit we just talked about got me really interested in X....'

Another alternative is to ask a question about your subject that has intrigued you and which has not been answered satisfactorily in your IB course. Showing interest and being positive is a good last impression to leave. But make sure to be genuine! These guys are incredibly good at sniffing out faux-interest and fakeness. And they don't want to endure those kinds of students for three whole years.

Pro Tip: Both Oxford and Cambridge have **websites that are packed with relevant information,** and you are strongly advised to read these carefully. You should also look for articles about applying to Oxbridge and this will help you build up a picture of what to expect.

Final Tips

- ✓ Show up early so that you are not late.
- ✓ Dress in comfortable but casually smart clothes. Shirt and trousers are fine.
- ✓ Do not answer monosyllabically but try to form coherent sentences. If you do not know the answer to a question, say so, but try to say something like 'I am afraid I'm not completely sure, but I would guess that...'
- ✓ Try not to sound too opinionated. Be objective and thoughtful, and open to changing your mind.

- ✓ Do not give the impression that you are well practiced with interviews and appear to be blasé / too nonchalant.
- ✓ Do arrange a practice interview with someone who knows the process, but don't overdo it. Just aim to be prepared to answer questions that you are not familiar with.
- ✓ Try to steer a discussion toward your 'comfort zone' of knowledge and experience.
- ✓ If you realize that you have said something stupid, try to save the situation by admitting it and offering an alternative.
- ✓ Be prepared for the predictable questions (e.g., why you chose this college / university).

Pro Tip: In the last decade or so, both universities have been willing to publish some sample questions that have been asked at interviews (and you can find even more online). See more recommended resources at the end of this chapter.

Here is a helpful article written by one of my students on how he got into the University of Cambridge:

Applying to the University of Cambridge

"Now that your school has given you an excellent predicted grade, or better still you've managed to achieve an outstanding score for the IB itself, you've just realized the world of possibilities that are now open to you. Spoiled for choice, you are looking at the sheer number of courses and universities you can apply to for your next phase in life. That was me, three years back after receiving my results, asking myself: *Should I go local? Should I go overseas? How does this whole process work?*

For those of you who managed to score well on the IB, you've probably considered applying to **Oxbridge**, where the standard entrance requirement for IB students is about 40–42 points with a 776 for your HLs depending on the course. Consistently ranked among the top universities internationally, with a strong support system for facilitating learning and tons of networking opportunities, I too, eventually decided to apply for a Law degree at the University of Cambridge.

Side note, if you didn't already know, between Oxford and Cambridge, you can only apply to one of them, not both. I picked Cambridge as their Law curriculum suited my needs more and in terms of comparing both towns, the vibes at Cambridge are way more lovely and charming compared to Oxford.[17]

Like applying to any other UK university, applying to Cambridge can only be done through the UCAS portal. The deadline for this is normally end of September, but I'd recommend you complete and submit your application weeks earlier as there are other steps to take after this. Also, Cambridge operates as a collegiate system, where it's made up of 31 colleges of different sizes, demographics, and specialties, but as a collective they make up Cambridge University. This means that on UCAS, you have to decide which college to apply to, or you can leave your application as "open" if you have no preference. After I submitted my UCAS application, I had to complete another application on Cambridge's website itself called COPA, meant for international applicants outside of the EU. In addition, I had to complete another form called the SAQ which the admissions team from Cambridge will email you. I understand that these administrative procedures can be quite confusing for some of you, but you can find out more on the university's website itself.

---

[17] This opinion is not shared by the authors of this book!

After managing to complete all the administrative procedures, I found myself awaiting the infamous interview and written test. Cambridge will normally dispatch an overseas admissions team to various places around the world at specific times to conduct their interviews and assessments for overseas applicants. Unfortunately, due to National Service commitments at the time, I could not make it for their interview and assessment in Singapore, so I had to travel to Mumbai for my own interview and assessment, with the kind support of my superiors and assistance of Cambridge's overseas admissions team. Should any of you who are serving the nation face a similar predicament as me, rest assured that their overseas admissions team will do their best to arrange something for you. They are just an email away!

I'm sure many of you have heard horror stories about the unorthodox questions they pose at the interview and the complex questions they throw at you in your subject specific written assessment. While this might be true, I mean I was asked how military occupations should be classified – in an interview which I thought was going to be law-related, don't be daunted by this. It's their way of seeing the way you process your thoughts and your first taste of what a supervision* will be like in Cambridge! I found myself engaged in topics I've never had the chance to think deeply about and having discussions with my interviewer on contentious issues. I didn't even notice that my interview time was up and found myself leaving the interview more intellectually stimulated than when I came in. As for the written test, the questions posed stumped me, and I had to scramble my thoughts and frantically piece together a somewhat coherent argument just before the time was up.

** Supervisions are one of the teaching methods in Cambridge where you can discuss your work and receive personal feedback from your supervisor who is probably a leading specialist in the field you are studying.*

Overall, like any other applicant aware of how competitive securing a spot in Cambridge is, I had doubts about getting an acceptance at all. When that decision email eventually came and I realized that I got accepted, I was very surprised and thankful of how the many things that could've gone wrong along the way did not. I'd sum up my experience in three takeaways:

1. Don't be daunted by how competitive and challenging the interview and assessment might be, treat it as a taster of what it is like to actually study in Cambridge. If you like it, great! It means their style of teaching will probably suit you. If not, don't be discouraged, we all have different styles of learning that we are more inclined to. There is probably another university out there that will vibe with you and facilitate your learning process better.

2. Keep your expectations open regardless of your feelings after the interview and assessment, don't beat yourself up because you felt or thought that it didn't go well. Your interviewer or assessor isn't there to "grade" your performance in the interview or written test like in the IB. They are there to see if you are compatible with the university's style of teaching and whether you have the potential to thrive in that specific environment.

3. Building on the second point, when you receive the decision email, if you got an offer, congrats! If you didn't, it doesn't make you less than any other applicant who got the offer. It might just mean that the admissions team thought that your academic potential could've been tapped to the fullest elsewhere instead of Cambridge. Ultimately, universities and their courses are just a means for us to acquire knowledge while building networks that we can tap into in the future. As long as you have that passion to learn and an unquenchable thirst for knowledge, nothing is going to stop you from attaining the goals you've set for yourself in the future.

Sample Questions

We have chosen a sample of questions that have been asked to Oxford college applicants here and added a description of what the questions intends to elicit.

Biological Sciences:

1. *Why do many animals have stripes?*

This is intended to generate discussion about potential advantages.

2. *If you could save either the rainforest or the coral reefs, which would you choose?*

This aims to test the interviewee's ability to present a coherent argument and identify a variety of impacts.

3. *Is it easier for organisms to live on land or in the sea?*

The interviewee must first consider the meaning of easier and then show an ability to assess relative problems.

4. *Would it matter if tigers became extinct?*

A 'yes' answer is expected but the 'why' is the most important part.

Biomedical Sciences:

1. *Why do cat's eyes appear to glow in the dark?*

The interviewee is expected to discuss possible advantages.

Engineering:

1. *How would you design a gravity dam for holding back water?*

This requires some technical ability to apply mathematics and physics.

English Literature:

1. *Why might it be useful for an English student to read the Twilight series?*

This is intended to test the interviewee's powers of literary analysis of non-exam texts.

Geography:

1. *If I were to visit the area where you live, what would I be interested in?*

This aims to test intellectual curiosity and ability to apply analytical concepts and awareness

History:

1. *Imagine we had no record of the past at all, except everything to do with sport (or drama, or music) how much of the past could we find out about?*

This aims to test the interviewee's use of imagination for linking familiar topic to historic research.

2. *Which person (or sort of person) in the past would you like to interview and why?*

This tests the interviewee's ability to match up the 'who' and 'why' appropriately.

Law:

1. *What does it mean for someone to 'take' another's car?*

This tests the interviewee's powers of reasoning and ability to consider hypothetical situations.

2. *If the punishment for parking on double yellow lines was death and therefore nobody did it, would that be a just and effective law?*

This tests the interviewee's recognition of different issues and ability to distinguish between just and effective.

Materials Science:

1. *How hot does the air in a hot air balloon have to be if I wanted to use it to lift an elephant?*

Here a correct answer is not expected. The aim is to test the interviewee's ability to identify important factors such as size, weight etc. and what mathematical techniques might be applied.

Medicine:

1. *Why does your heart rate increase when you exercise?*

This question aims to elicit the simple answer regarding oxygen and then test more deeply with follow-up questions.

2. *Why do we have red blood cells?*

This question is looking for a wider understanding beyond the basics.

The questions listed above provide the general idea of what the interviewers are looking for. There is rarely a correct or incorrect answer, and most questions aim to test the ability of the candidate to apply knowledge, think laterally and identify interesting possibilities. The advice to all candidates is to relax and face the interview with an open mind. Do not over-prepare but do have some practice as a test run.

Both Oxford and Cambridge provide videos of parts of an interview on their websites and a Google search will provide examples of mock interviews for certain subjects. These might be helpful, but do not obsess about the interview. Have an idea of what to expect but remember it is important to have a fresh open mind that can engage with the unfamiliar and the unexpected.

CHAPTER 7

MEDICINE

This chapter is again written with the UK-bound applicant in mind, however much of this information will be useful for applying to medicine in other parts of Europe.

IB applicants for medicine are sometimes at a slight disadvantage because their school only allows them to take two science subjects, which will inevitably be Biology and Chemistry.

Pro Tip: If you plan on pursuing Medicine, you basically **need to take HL Biology and HL Chemistry**

Some medical schools prefer applicants to have Physics, as well. A-Level applicants will typically offer these three subjects at A-Level, together with A-Level Math. You should however, be aware that you can get special permission to take three science subjects if you are applying for medicine. Alternatively, you could take a GCSE in Physics or sit for the A-Level or AS-Level. You might consider one of these alternatives if you want to strengthen your application, but it is by no means essential. Many IB applicants have been accepted for medicine with just Higher-Level Biology and Chemistry and Standard Level Math.

Some medical schools even prefer candidates to have a wider breadth of subjects, including social science and humanities. Before applying, you should check the university prospectus and the entry requirements. If you are still in doubt, contact the department, either by email or phone, to ask what their policy is regarding subjects offered and if they have a preferred combination. You should also check whether they require additional tests like UKCAT. If so, make sure you do some practice questions.

The grades required for medicine are not excessively high and will normally be in the range of 35 to 39. What is crucial is a personal statement that clearly shows your desire to study medicine and your suitability for the course. Many applicants will have taken a gap year to gain suitable work experience. Although extremely advantageous, it is not essential to work with 'Doctors Without Borders' in Africa or something similar. Helping out in a local clinic or hospital or old people's home is also valuable and acceptable.

You should not just list these experiences, but you should discuss them with respect to how it impacted on you and your desire to study medicine as well as confirming your suitability for the course.

> **Pro Tip:** If you do not take a gap year you will not necessarily be disadvantaged, but **you should still have some suitable work experience gained at weekends or during holidays.** Try to give a realistic reason for wanting to study medicine or dentistry.

Having parents or family who are doctors is a good reason and it can link up convincingly with your awareness of what the training involves and the sacrifices that have to be made. If this is not the case, it would be sensible to refer to your work experience and the satisfaction you received. It would be inappropriate to say that the medical profession will offer you a high salary and a good job prospect, even though this might be your true motivation. A particular experience of a family illness or accident might be what stimulated your interest but if this is the case, you must be careful not to sound too melodramatic.

An alternative is to describe an interest in medical research and the prospect of adapting new technology and developments. You will need to be able to show knowledge of new breakthroughs and techniques and so reading contemporary journals is essential.

Your personal statement has to show your interest in the subject and your suitability and experience. Your academic interests are also important and you should state any particular field of interest, such as genetics or stem cell propagation, that you might have. In addition, a brief mention of your other interests is useful, such as music or dance or riding. You might even refer to their potential therapeutic attributes. The selectors will be looking for a well-rounded individual who also has interests outside the field of medicine. Your extracurricular activities can also be used to show your leadership qualities and commitment. You need to show an awareness of the hard work involved in completing a medical degree and your capacity for this.

With a good personal statement, a good reference and convincing work experience, there is a good chance that you will be called for an interview.

Pro Tip: Don't take HL Math AA unless you absolutely need to. It is very time consuming, difficult and you may struggle with your other priorities.

The Medicine Interview

An interview for Medicine is likely to be rather more specific than those outlined in the previous section. Although some questions will be of a general nature, the majority will be more knowledge-based aiming to test your understanding of biology and chemistry, as well as your medical perception.

You will be asked about your personal statement and your work experience and you need to be convincing in your responses showing how you have benefitted from the experiences that you have described. You need to display compassion and empathy with patients, while at the same time showing strength and willpower to overcome emotion. Describing personal experiences from your work or volunteer service will enable you to convey these attributes.

Be prepared for questions such as why you have selected medicine instead of nursing. Your reply should not in any way belittle nursing as a profession and you should provide good reasons for wanting to become a doctor. An interest in medical research or surgery could be a possible valid reason. Bear in mind that many of the reasons you might give for wanting to become a doctor would apply equally well to nursing.

You should be prepared to answer questions relating to medical ethics and to express an opinion on issues such as cloning, euthanasia and abortion. You might be presented with hypothetical situations to judge how you would act or react; for example, if the parents of a child refused to allow you to perform a lifesaving blood transfusion on religious grounds. It would also be an advantage to have some knowledge of the **British National Health Service (NHS)** as it is currently undergoing important review and funding assessment. If you are a non-UK applicant, some knowledge of your own country's health system would be advisable. You should also have some idea of how to assess a national health system and be able to identify strengths and weaknesses.

Unlike other interviews, which mainly concentrate on establishing academic ability and powers of analysis, the interviewers for medicine will also be interested in your body language and temperament. A degree of timidity and anxiety will be expected, but to become a successful doctor you must be decisive and able to inspire confidence in patients. Your potential bedside manner will be under scrutiny, as well as your character and charisma. You must express yourself clearly and try to display a thoughtful and amiable disposition. Above all you must be sincere and eager to embark on this demanding profession. The way that you present your personal experiences is clearly going to be an important factor in demonstrating your suitability. Finding yourself in a difficult situation says nothing about you, what is important is how you deal with the situation and what you learn from it.

Some universities are increasingly favoring a technique known as **Multiple Mini Interviews** (MMI) where the candidate is taken round a circuit and presented with a variety of situations, some real and some with actors. The aim is to allow for a more objective assessment of your reactions and to limit the advantage that interview preparation may have for private school applicants. By presenting a variety of situations, it gives candidates a chance to compensate for a bad performance in one situation and provides the basis for an objective overall evaluation of their suitability. The questions that are presented do not have a right or wrong answer but, as with the Oxbridge formula, you are judged on how you react to the situations. The questions are likely to be of a general nature and do not necessarily involve medical knowledge, but rather will test your handling of the situation. According to Sara Doherty, of St. Georges University "It's a practical assessment...Candidates have to show us what they're capable of doing, rather than tell us."

It remains to be seen whether this style of interview will replace the traditional type or whether any new style will be developed. Whatever the interview form, it is likely that the aim will be to test the traditional values of motivation, ethics, empathy, and decisive communication skills.

Most universities provide detailed information in their prospectus and websites about the whole selection procedure and students are recommended to conduct exhaustive research before finalizing their application.

Cardiff University presents the following information for potential applicants:

- ❖ In the 2017 intake, the University received more than 2,450 applications for 309 places; of these approximately 900 were invited for interview.
- ❖ Applicants who meet the minimum academic requirements are assessed on non-academic criteria according to the information contained in their personal statement and the referee's report.
- ❖ Applications are reviewed by trained selectors and the following are assessed and scored: Medical motivation and awareness of the career.
- ❖ Caring ethos and a sense of social awareness Sense of responsibility. Evidence of a balanced approach to life. Evidence of self-directed learning and extracurricular activities.
- ❖ All applicants are expected to have an appreciation of the length of the training program and the career structure.
- ❖ No offers are made without interview. Interviews are offered to applicants who achieve the highest positions according to their academic and non-academic rankings (some degree of mutual compensation between these is allowed). The number of applicants to be interviewed in order to meet the student intake quota is determined at the start of the admissions cycle.

- Interviews normally take place during a four-month period beginning in November, and no significance should be attached to whether the interview date is early or late within this period.

- Those who are not invited for interview will be informed, through UCAS, that their application has been unsuccessful.

- Interviews normally last 20 minutes.

- The composition of the University's team of interviewers recognizes the importance of balance in terms of gender and ethnicity as well as covering a range of professions associated with medicine. Each interview panel is drawn from this team and normally consists of 2 or 3 interviewers, at least one of whom is medically qualified, unless exceptional circumstances prevent the clinician attending. Panels may include a medical student from the senior years. Interviewers receive specific training and guidance on the form and conduct of the interview, including issues relating to equal opportunities and the benefits of diversity.

- The aim of the interview is to explore the non-academic criteria (see above) and to encourage applicants to talk naturally about themselves, their studies, and their experiences, and to demonstrate that they have the interpersonal skills to be able to communicate effectively and whether they have a balanced approach to life. In this way they can show how they meet the academic and non-academic attributes required of a prospective doctor.

- Individual interviewers assess each applicant's performance and the interviewer panel agrees an overall recommendation.

- The final decision to offer a place is made by the Admissions Sub-Committee Selection Panel, chaired by the Sub-Dean for Admissions. It is determined by an applicant's overall ranking, based on a combination of the academic profile, personal statement and referee's report, and the interview performance.

Most medical schools will operate a similar selection process, though there might be variations in emphasis and selection criteria. Any such differences should be detailed in the prospectus and the website.

How to Manage IB and Apply for Medicine

It is rather daunting to balance those six subjects of IB plus the Extended Essay and TOK with medicine application (UCAT, BMAT and interviews). Many would fret over which should be given higher priority: is it the medicine application, because if you don't get in, then getting fantastic results in the IB does not seem so useful? Or is it the IB, since you need to meet the conditional offers that medical schools give you?

I would say they are both important but depending on the point of time you are in; you can give priority to one over the other. A brief time plan should give you this:

UCAT: July to October

UCAS deadline: mid-October

BMAT: September or November

IB Coursework: (variable due to internal deadlines set by schools) generally, January to March

IB Exam: May (or Nov)

One might notice that the summer after Lower Sixth would hold much importance. So, whilst ideally, one would use that summer to de-stress, relax and remove the toxins accumulated after one school year, your post-lower-sixth summer should instead be put to good use revising for UCAT, BMAT, planning for personal statements and brainstorming ideas for extended essay and various pieces of coursework. It does sound like hard work but few tips to make it relatively durable:

1. **Divide the workload into easy-to-manage chunks.**

Don't cram all the revision in one day. Do a few questions per day and of course, nearer to the UCAT or BMAT, do try to do the whole thing under timed conditions.

The same applies to IB revision.

2. **Remember quality, not quantity.**

In those time chunks that you allocate to a subject, don't focus on getting through as many questions as you can, but getting it correct. Try to get to the crux of why you got a question wrong, as a similar framework or thinking approach can be utilized for other questions. Good resources for these would be the UCAT and BMAT question banks offered by 6med, the UCAT ninja and BMAT ninja respectively. You might also want to enroll yourself in a 6med UCAT/BMAT crash course to get some guidance and top tips.

3. **Set deadlines.**

Set your own internal deadline to complete the task. For instance, the deadline for personal statement is mid-October (the time when you need to submit your UCAS), you might want to set your deadline of submitting UCAS to early October, which means you should complete your personal statement by late August to give yourself plenty of time to give to your supervisors or friends to comment and for you to correct.

So, with UCAT, UCAS, BMAT and coursework out of the way, you can then focus on interviews and the Final IB Exam. Again, a similar approach can be used. However, with the added complexity of IB exam being 6 subjects with 2-3 papers each, another useful tip would be to spice things up by swapping subjects when you start to get bored or lose attention. E.g., Why not do a Math past paper when you get bored of revising for Chemistry?

Final Tips

The following are some tips from a student of mine who recently got accepted to medicine at Kings:

UKCAT

The UKCAT is quite important when it comes to applying for Medical School, and the schools which I applied to valued the UKCAT relatively highly (King's, St. George's, Birmingham) in their assessment of applications, so I knew that this mattered a lot for me (but depending on where you apply it has relative amounts of importance). It's a bit unfair because you only get one shot at this, and a factor to doing well is how hard the questions actually are on the day. The resource that I would recommend using is Medify, it is decently priced and is 100% worth the money. There is an absolutely ridiculous amount of questions on that website, as well as a series of practice tests which are very useful to do. Only begin to do those closer to your exam time when you want a feel for the actual exam and how it works. The UKCAT Consortium website has a few practice tests which you could do as well. For the verbal reasoning section, you just need to read quite a bit before and increase your reading speed, and read the question before the text, so that you are only looking for answers, you don't have time to read extensively. For quantitative reasoning you just want to get used to the calculator, which Medify has on all of their questions, so you can build up your speed on the calculator, and in the actual exam use Number Lock. For decision making, you just want to get used to the types of questions which are given on the exam and build up your speed when answering them. Abstract reasoning was a section which confused me for so long, until I learned about looking out for SCANS (Shape, Color, Arrangement, Number, Symmetry) which made life a lot easier. To build your speed at looking for these features, you just need to do exam questions under timed conditions. To study for situational judgement, you want to read over the condensed versions of Tomorrow's Doctors and apply those principles to all of the questions because those are the ethical principles which doctors in the NHS use.

BMAT

This exam is just really hard in my opinion, like incredibly difficult, but Medify again is a really good resource to revise for this. For Section 1, what it takes is just a hell of a lot of practice, and Medify, the free past papers provided by Cambridge online and BMAT Ninja can provide. The types of questions can repeat at times (such as elevator questions associated with time), so doing past papers to build up your speed and learning the styles of questions can be incredibly helpful for this. This section is not too time pressured so you actually have time to read, just be aware of common traps, such as reading graph axes properly, and reading units on tables correctly so that you do not lose easy marks here. Section 2 is so damn time pressured, and for this reason, read the syllabus, and learn all of the points so that you can recall them in a couple of seconds as soon as you have seen the question. Again, Medify and the free past papers online can help you with doing this but you need to learn everything and learn it really well. Past papers help to learn some of the common topics which come up, such as Energetic for chemistry, pedigree charts and family trees for Biology and circuit questions for Physics, and once you practice these questions you learn to do them a lot quicker. For Section 3, the best way to start revising is reading the condensed version of Tomorrow's Doctors and knowledge into one document which you can memorize info from. From here, if you use Medify, look at the past papers to collect some real-world examples there which you can talk about in your essay more, and simply memorize this information. Luckily, most of the universities which require the BMAT usually need around a 3A so you do not need to include too much complex information in your essay, but it just needs to be structured and written very well to ensure that you get an A for quality of writing. Imperial was the BMAT university that I had applied to, and I scored highly enough on the BMAT to receive an interview, and I would credit Medify completely for helping to get me the BMAT score which was necessary. Last thing, one of the universities which I was thinking of applying to required people to take the BMAT in October, so I took it in October, but if you know what BMAT university you want to apply to, get it done in September so that you have your score before you apply. Oh, another more thing, this applies to all Medical applicants: WATCH ALI ABDAAL VIDEOS! This guy is an absolute legend when it comes to admissions test advice and interview advice (even revision strategies!)

Panel Interviews & MMIs

For the university that I had applied to that did panel interviews (Imperial), the way it worked was that there would be three people who would just bombard you with questions for about twenty minutes (really intimidating!), plus a lay observer. Each university varies in their style, even for MMIs, so read things like The Student Room and the university's website to see how they run their interviews. For Imperial, they gave some generic points on what areas they like to assess in each candidate, and for the universities that I had applied to, they all did this, so I would write down those points on a piece of paper and think of all possible questions they could form on each of those main points and how you would respond to them. This technique usually works as there is only so much that a university could possibly question you about. In addition to doing this, I would purchase a book called Medical School Interviews (2nd Edition). Over 150 Questions Analyzed, by ISC Medical, because it is an absolute godsend which takes pretty much any possible interview question that you could be asked about and gives you a strong and weak response to those questions so you can see how to approach it. If you get this book, for MMIs the only other extra work you would have to do, other than reading this and practicing the questions with a mate/family member (DO NOT MEMORISE ANSWERS, no matter how tempting it seems), is research your university and think about why you applied there and formulate a good answer as to why you want to study Medicine, and why Medicine at this university suits you (make sure you try to relate your answers back to Medicine or the university, even if the questions aren't Medicine related), because a lot of the examiners like to see people doing this.

I want to make a separate point on two things: Ethics & Mock scenarios (which the book I referenced earlier provides), because many universities like to ask about one, if not both, of these, because it shows how you approach situations under incredibly high pressure (practicing it is the only thing which can make this feel less uncomfortable). I regret not spending more time on the Ethics based revision (know of mis-practices (Bawa-Garba case, Charlie-Gard case, Harold Shipman case, etc.) & current Medical news too, as you can be asked about these (brexit's effect on the NHS, the slight increase in the NHS budget, etc.)) because my response to the ethics based question at Imperial is what got me a rejection from there when I asked for feedback. So, in the rest of my interviews, I spent so much more time on it (the ISC Medical book helps with it), and I managed to get offers, but I really regret not nailing down those situations from the start. If you are really confused on an ethics-based question, think about the four pillars of Medical ethics: Autonomy, Beneficence, Non-Maleficence & Justice, and link your responses back to these. For other universities, just make sure that you practice some other skills such as analyzing graphs, as I got asked about this at one of my MMIs (KNOW THE DIFFERENCE BETWEEN DESCRIBE AND EXPLAIN), and it is an easy station to score full marks on. Another good way of revising would be to watch simulated doctor-patient scenarios, and analyze your thoughts on them, which the ISC Medical Interview book teaches you how to do. If you learn how to do this, and you get asked about it in one of your MMIs, it is a really easy station to nail completely. Just some more general thoughts which came to my mind about MMIs are that do not panic if one station goes worse than you would've liked. Many of the examiners are assessing independently and are instructed not to interact with one another after to keep the situation as unbiased as possible and talk to other applicants when you get there, it gets you in the mood of talking and puts you a bit more at ease.

CHAPTER 8

UNITED STATES

This chapter will provide a brief introduction to the American higher education system and its application process.[18] We will also provide some specific advice for IB students.

Introduction

More than 4,500 accredited institutions make up higher education in the US. Unlike in many countries, US higher education institutions are not centrally organized or managed but are autonomous and accredited by independent regional bodies.

Bachelor's Degrees

[18] **Adapted from** https://www.ibo.org/contentassets/5895a05412144fe890312bad52b17044/recognition---international-student-guide-us--march2016---eng.pdf.pdf

The bachelor's degree is the main undergraduate degree type at US universities and colleges. It is usually completed in four years of full-time study and is awarded after completing a specified number of credits in a major field. Students typically earn credits for courses they take, and these credits count towards the completion of a program. Every course earns a certain number of credits, and each institution has its own requirement for the number of credits needed to graduate.

State colleges and universities, also called public institutions, were founded, and subsidized by US state governments to provide a low-cost education to residents of that state. Public universities generally offer access to research opportunities and classes in a wide variety of fields of study. Because of the high number of faculty research grants, public institutions tend to have large departments offering a variety of degrees. These institutions tend to be very large and, because of government subsidies, are typically less expensive to attend than private institutions.

Private institutions receive the majority or entirety of their funding from alumni donations, faculty research grants and tuition fees. This typically makes them more expensive to attend but allows for more resources available to students.

Liberal arts institutions offer courses in the arts, humanities, languages, mathematics, and social and physical sciences. The majority of liberal arts institutions are private.

Associate Degrees

Community and technical colleges are another option that provides two-year associate degree programs to prepare students to continue studies for an undergraduate degree or help them gain occupational skills for immediate employment. These institutions generally accept most students who apply, regardless of previous academic performance.

Most community colleges have articulation agreements with the public universities in the same state; students can complete their general studies at a community college and, if they meet minimum performance standards, transfer to a four-year institution to complete the remaining two years of their bachelor's degree. Community colleges are an excellent choice for students who did not earn the IB diploma but wish to study in the US.

Groups and Leagues

Many universities are included within popular groups of other institutions. Often these groupings form out of similarities in academic reputation, selectivity, or athletic conference. Ivy League institutions, for example, are eight institutions in the northeast region of the US that compete in the same athletic conference; academically, they typically all rank in the top 15 universities in the US. The Ivy League has connotations of academic excellence, selectivity in admissions and social elitism. The University of California (UC) is an example of a public state system. Comprised of ten university campuses throughout the state, UC refers to California's public research universities that offer doctoral degrees. Although each campus is considered selective, the relative selectivity varies between them. The UC has some system-wide admissions requirements and recognition/benefits for IB students, but individual campuses may have additional policies. University rankings. No official ranking system exists for colleges and universities in the US, although there are independent bodies that conduct subjective rankings annually. US universities are commonly ranked among the highest globally, and in most international university rankings the US is the country with the largest number of highly ranked institutions.

The Application Process

Contact

US institutions are autonomous, and students must apply to each institution directly. In addition, application procedures and requirements may vary considerably from one institution to another. The Common Application is a not-for-profit member organization that allows students to apply to more than 600 institutions through a single application process, although some institutions might still have additional requirements beyond the Common Application. The popularity is growing, but there are still many universities and colleges that do not use the Common Application.

Pro Tip: The US, more than most other regions, places a huge emphasis on extracurricular and non-academic factors. I've seen students who were rather average academically get into great schools because they just stood out on their applications.

Choosing an area of study

At liberal arts institutions, unless a student chooses a very specific area of study (such as pre-medicine or engineering) a major is typically not required until partway through the undergraduate degree. Thus, students usually do not need to indicate their preferred area of study when applying. The first one to two years of the degree will have general education requirements, allowing students to gain broader exposure to a range of faculties before choosing a major to focus the remainder of their courses on.

Pro Tip: Each US university will really have a different admissions policy. You need to look on their websites or call the admissions office to ask to see what their specific policies are.

The application

Admissions offices at US institutions tend to look at student performance holistically, taking a variety of factors into consideration in addition to academic performance. Each institution has its own admissions standards and evaluation process. There is no national university entrance exam, but many institutions will require SAT or ACT exam scores. Many applications can be completed online, and most applications will require biographical information and education background (including school transcripts and IB predicted grades). It is also common for institutions to request letters of recommendation, personal essays, test scores or proof of English proficiency. Students should find out what an application requires well in advance of the application deadline.

Pro Tip: Make sure to check the common application website: https://www.commonapp.org/

Timeline

It is important to check the application deadline for each institution, as deadlines may vary, but many are in December or January. Because the US admissions cycle happens prior to the May IB exam session, US institutions base their admissions decisions on anticipated IB scores reported by the student's school in conjunction with the other factors listed above. Generally, after an offer is made, students are required to verify that the predicted results used for admissions decisions were accurate by requesting the IB send their exam results to the institution. Many institutions will accept the IB transcript as a school-leaving credential, but some may require a separate high school diploma as well.

Pro Tip: The offers from US universities for IB students are almost always 'unconditional'.

IB Students

Nearly all higher education institutions in the US will consider performance in the IB Diploma Program (DP) for the purpose of admissions or other factors including granting course credit, advanced standing, scholarships, or financial aid.

Admissions requirements

Most institutions do not set minimum required scores for IB students. They prefer to take into account a combination of course selection and performance, extended essay and creativity, activity, service activities, interviews or personal statements, letters of recommendation, and often performance on other standardized exams. Additionally, many US institutions look at performance in individual IB courses rather than the collective point total. It is important to keep in mind that selectivity varies greatly between institutions. While most will consider the IB as a pathway, some institutions will expect exemplary performance in their applicants. Other institutions will admit IB applicants with a wide range of scores. Admissions requirements are often not spelled out clearly in IB terms on university websites and vary from institution to institution. It is recommended to speak directly with a university representative to gain a clearer understanding of what level of performance will be likely to gain entry.

Pro Tip: Your college essays are very important. Start them soon and make sure you have a good 'story'.

Benefits

Many US higher education institutions offer benefits to IB students. Benefits are determined by each institution individually, but might include credit for certain IB scores, scholarships, or tuition assistance. Some universities allow IB students to enter their institution as second-year students, meaning the undergraduate education will be three years instead of four.

DP Course students

Students taking DP courses but not the full diploma might be able to receive credit from institutions for individual courses, but policy is also determined by each institution, and sometimes each individual program or faculty within the institution. Some institutions indicate their IB recognition policy on their website.

Anticipated grades

It is important to note that the admissions cycle in the US takes place before IB students even sit exams. Thus, admissions decisions are often based in part on the student's anticipated grades submitted by the school. If a student's final IB scores are significantly below the anticipated grades submitted by the school, it is possible for the university to withdraw its offer. As such, it is vital that teachers and schools report students' anticipated grades as accurately as possible. This is not only important for students' futures, but if a school consistently inflates anticipated grades, it may tarnish that school's reputation with the university.

Do IB final grades matter for US university admissions?

Here is what some of my US students had to say when I asked them the question, 'do final IB grades matter for US university admissions?':

"Short answer: No. Long answer: No but let me explain. During your junior year of high school (second to last year if you aren't

familiar with the high school year system) you take ACT or SAT tests which are the tests universities need in order to figure out if you are a good enough candidate for them. After getting your desired score or getting the desired score for your university, you then have to apply online. Usually, the application process is putting your school information, your family information, if you took any college courses during the summer (called Dual Enrollment and I'm not sure if you guys have a similar thing), and all that good stuff. Usually, but not always, you have to write a short (maybe a max of 500 words) about a prompt that they give you. During the whole application process, they never ask about your IB scores but they do ask if you took IB, AP, Honors, or any other type of classes."

"The university can technically rescind acceptance if there's a discrepancy between predicted and actual grades but realistically, they won't. It's in their interest to take your money."

*"Universities in US don't give a **** about the IB. Around ¼ of DP students sit exams in US, and most of them will have received offers a month before their exams and committed a day before exams. As long as you pass the IB and graduate high school with all credits and graduation requirements completed, there's practically no way a US university will rescind your application. That is, unless you mess up big time and fail your final year courses. Extra tip: they may not need your IB score or even if you got your IB diploma. However, the really cool thing is even if you pass some of your exams or if you didn't get the diploma, they still give you college credit for the exams you took. At least that's how my university works."*

However, when it comes to Predicted Grades, it may not be so. After the Harvard Asian American lawsuit[19], a lot of Harvard's internal admissions procedures were made public and this provides the proof that US universities do look at predicted grades. This is a

---

[19] https://en.wikipedia.org/wiki/Students_for_Fair_Admissions_v._President_and_Fellows_of_Harvard_College

direct quote from Harvard's class of 2018 reading procedures manual "In the absence of final marks, use predicted marks. If predicted marks are not available, use internal grades".[20] Although we can't say all universities look at Predicted Grades in the same way, the most public example of an extremely esteemed school seems to suggest that Predicted Grades are important.

Who Applies to the US?

In 2014, 759 U.S. institutions received 9,0161 transcripts from 8,163 overseas students (although around a quarter of these students hold American passports). This averages 1.1 transcripts per student, suggesting that most students send transcripts to only one institution. It can be assumed that students who sent transcripts to US institutions were admitted to those institutions, as by the time IB results are released, students generally know which university they plan to attend. Transcripts were sent from a variety of countries. Even the most common countries of origin, China, and India, only account for 12% and 11%, respectively, of the total number of transcripts sent to US institutions from abroad. Six of the ten most common origin countries are from the Asia-Pacific region, with places such as Thailand and Indonesia sending numbers comparable with those of the UK.

[20] https://www.politico.com/f/?id=00000166-9690-d166-a77e-9f9c92f10001

Most common source of transcripts coming into the US

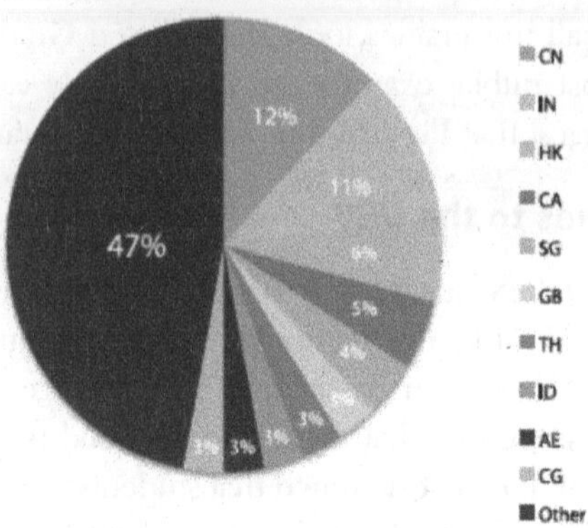

Where do IB students Apply?

Students send transcripts to a very wide variety of institutions. Even the 50 most popular institutions received just over half (4,939) of transcripts sent to the US. Of these 50, 19 are public institutions, with University of California campuses accounting for six. From these 50 institutions:

- eight are in California
- seven are in Massachusetts
- five are in New York
- nine are in the mid-west: Illinois, Indiana, Michigan, Ohio, Wisconsin
- seven are in the northeast: Connecticut, Pennsylvania, New Jersey, Rhode Island
- six are in the southeast: Florida, Georgia, North Carolina
- five are in the mid-east: Washington, DC, Maryland, Virginia
- three are in the west: Colorado, Texas, Washington.

The 10 institutions that received the largest number of transcripts account for 25% of all transcripts sent to the US. Half are public and half are private. Seven of the 10 are ranked as top 100 universities by the QS World University ranking.

Pro Tip: Really look into the environment of the university you're considering and see if it matches with what you want to get out of college.

US University Profiles

US universities evaluate academic grades in the context of a student's high school curriculum and its degree of rigor. The two-year IB Diploma Program is widely regarded as an academically demanding syllabus, and one that provides excellent preparation for college level coursework.

Pro Tip: Do not simply assume that you have a huge advantage over non-IB kids in your application. You have to actually make your IB experience work in your favor in the application.

A **survey of more than 4,000 students** conducted by the International Insight Research Group in partnership with the International Baccalaureate Organization (IBO) showed that the acceptance rate of IB students into Ivy League universities is up to 18% higher than the total population acceptance rate. The gap is even more significant for top-ranked universities outside of the Ivy League, where it is **22% higher**.

This document draws on these survey results to compare the general population acceptance rate to the IB Diploma student acceptance rate at the top 25 US universities, so you can see where an IB qualification will give your application the biggest boost. Unlike their UK counterparts, US universities don't release official cut-off scores for the IB Diploma. Based on what the Oxbridge universities in the UK expect from IB applicants, an overall grade of 38+ would be well received by the Ivy Leagues. For the more selective universities, you're looking at around 40+. This doesn't mean that you won't be accepted if you score below 38 or get a less than perfect grade in one of your subjects. It simply means that a 38+ is viewed favorably by the university. There are many other factors that go into a university application, and admissions officers assess them holistically.

Pro Tip: One of my biggest tips for US applications is to try to be as diversified as possible. Good scores will only get you so far, so be sure to have a balance of solid scores and a plethora of activities, clubs and extracurriculars.

One thing is for sure: by taking the IB Diploma, you automatically rise to the top of the admissions pool. US colleges love good grades, but what they love even more is to see that you've pushed yourself to get them. Universities appreciate the IB's rigor and they know it takes hard work and dedication to perform well, particularly in Higher Level (HL) subjects.

Pro Tip: Predicted grades will not really give you an advantage over those who do not do IB (the college basically wants to see that you took the hardest courses available to you).

This is demonstrated by the fact that most US universities award course credits for IB Diploma subjects. The more generous a university is with its credit distribution, the more it loves IB students (and the more likely admissions officers are to admit you!).

Competitive IB Scores at US universities

We spent some time emailing US universities to get a feel for their average IB scores and we got some very straightforward responses:

USC - *"students applying with a predicted 36 or 37 out of 42 are competitive in the process"*

University of Michigan - *"Most competitive students in IB programs generally have predicted scores in the mid to high 30s on the 45-point final exam."*

Fordham - *"The average IB score for admitted students is typically in the low to mid 30s. Often students receive a mix of results of 5 to 6."*

Boston College - *"We give a recommended range of 35 points and above, which includes consideration of the IB courses a student has selected"*

Georgie Tech - *"Students should have mostly scores of 6 and 7. Higher Level Math and Sciences courses are encouraged but not required to be competitive for admission."*

Penn State - "*Most students admitted to University Park have more 6s and 7s than 5s. The other 19 campuses where you can do the 2+2 program (2 years at a campus 2 years at University Park) are less competitive and we see more of a mix of 5s and some 4s"*

Wake Forest - *"Our admitted applicants usually have predicted scores of 5, 6, or 7 in each subject."*

UW Madison - *"Competitive applicants receive scores of 5-7 on their IB subject exams"*

Dartmouth - *"The bulk of our students are scoring on the high end of the test range"*

Popular University Choices:

Here are the profiles of the 10 most popular US colleges for IB students along with additional information on admission requirements and credit:

BOSTON UNIVERSITY		
General admissions information[5]		
When reviewing your high school/secondary school transcript, Boston University looks at a variety of factors, including overall level of achievement; enrollment in honours, AP or IB-level courses; and your individual academic strengths.	Total undergraduate enrollment[6]	17k
	Overall acceptance rate[7]	46%
	Global ranking[8]	91
	Average DP score[9]	34
Credit and advanced standing		
Higher level (HL) courses passed with a grade of 5 or higher may receive 8 credits. Credit for additional DP exams subject to approval.		

NEW YORK UNIVERSITY		
General admissions information		
To be eligible for admission, applicants are expected to submit results from one of the following testing options: • The SAT Reasoning Test • The ACT with Writing Test • Three SAT Subject Test scores • Three AP exam scores • The IB diploma • Three IB HL exam scores (if you are not an IB diploma candidate	Total undergraduate enrollment	24k
	Overall acceptance rate	26%
	Global ranking	53
	Average DP score	36
Credit and advanced standing		
HL examinations passed with grades of 6 or 7 may be considered for credit and/or placement depending on the area of study and/or programme requirements. Typically, eight semester hours of credit (equivalent to two terms or one academic year of a specific subject) will be awarded for each HL examination meeting the requirements of New York University.		
Additional considerations		
SAT/ACT exams are optional.		

NORTHEASTERN UNIVERSITY		
General admissions information		
For students applying from schools outside of the US, the SAT and ACT are not required. However, for applicants interested in presenting the most competitive application, Northeastern strongly encourages applicants to submit one of the following: AP exam results, a full IB diploma, three HL IB exam scores, or the results from nationally or regionally accredited exams that signify completion of secondary education.	**Total undergraduate enrollment**	14k
	Overall acceptance rate	32%
	Global ranking	365
	Average DP score	32
Credit and advanced standing		
Northeastern accepts scores of 5, 6, or 7 on most HL exams for credit.		

PENNSYLVANIA STATE UNIVERSITY–UNIVERSITY PARK*		
General admissions information		
In reviewing an application, we look for students who have successfully completed courses or examinations in the core subjects of mathematics, physical science, social science and language in all years of high school. Penn State requires first-year international students to submit an official score from the SAT or ACT examination.	**Total undergraduate enrollment**	39k
	Overall acceptance rate	54%
	Global ranking	101
	Average DP score	32
Credit and advanced standing		
Penn State will award transfer credit for exams taken at HL in which students have received a 5 or above.		
Additional considerations		
International students whose native language is not English must submit proof of English language proficiency. A score of 5 or higher on the English A: Language and literature (SL/HL) exam fulfills this requirement.		

PURDUE UNIVERSITY–WEST LAFAYETTE*		
General admissions information		
Those who pursue the strongest-possible college preparatory programme and take advantage of any available HL International Baccalaureate (IB) or honours courses generally are more competitive candidates for admission and more qualified to succeed in college.	**Total undergraduate enrollment**	29k
	Overall acceptance rate	60%
	Global ranking	89
	Average DP score	34
Credit and advanced standing		
Credit will normally be awarded for scores of 5–7 in HL subjects only, but there are a few exceptions. Students with lower grades might be able to test out of those subjects.		
Additional considerations		
Students interested in applying for technical programmes (engineering, science, health-related majors, technology and agriculture, etc) should take as much advanced coursework as possible in math and science (IB calculus [sic], IB biology, IB chemistry and IB physics).		

UNIVERSITY OF CALIFORNIA - BERKELEY

General admissions information

Admission to UC Berkeley is a two-step process: satisfying college and major requirements and selection. All achievement—both academic and non-academic/personal—is considered in the context of your educational circumstances, with an emphasis on the opportunities or challenges presented to you and your response to them. No single attribute or characteristic guarantees the admission of any applicant to Berkeley.		
	Total undergraduate enrollment	27k
	Overall acceptance rate	18%
	Global ranking	26
	Average DP score	38

Credit and advanced standing

Students who complete the IB diploma with a score of 30 or above will receive 30 quarter (20 semester) units toward their UC degree. Students who receive IB certificates with scores of 5, 6 or 7 on HL exams will receive 8 quarter (5.3 semester) units.

Additional considerations

Designated examinations are awarded elective units that may be applied to UC graduation requirements for specific subjects and/or for general education/breadth requirements, as determined by each campus.

UNIVERSITY OF CALIFORNIA–LOS ANGELES

General admissions information

UCLA receives the most applications of any university in the US. All applications are read twice. All academic and non-academic/personal achievement is considered in the context of your educational circumstances, with an emphasis on the opportunities or challenges presented to you and your response to them. No single attribute or characteristic guarantees the admission of any applicant. Students enrolled in IB World Schools are expected to earn scores of 5 or higher on HL exams, and most admitted students typically score 38+ points on the IB diploma.		
	Total undergraduate enrollment	28k
	Overall acceptance rate	22%
	Global ranking	27
	Average DP score	38

Credit and advanced standing

UCLA awards college credit for most HL exams with scores of 5 or higher. (We do not award college credit for standard level exams.) The specific credit you receive depends on the college/school your major belongs to.

UNIVERSITY OF CALIFORNIA–SAN DIEGO

General admissions information

International students must have completed secondary school with a superior average in academic subjects and have earned a certificate of completion that enables the student to be admitted to a university in the home country. If you are completing your IB diploma or taking some IB courses, make sure to report your IB status in your application.		
	Total undergraduate enrollment	23k
	Overall acceptance rate	38%
	Global ranking	44
	Average DP score	35

Credit and advanced standing

UCSD grants exemptions or credit for scores of 5–7 in many HL courses. Only HL exams are accepted for credit. Scores of 6 or 7 on standard level English exam meets UC Entry Level Writing requirement but no unit credit is granted. IB students can earn a maximum of 30 credits for their scores.

Additional considerations

Please request that internal marks and intermediate results/certificates from your school or appropriate authority are sent to UC San Diego by July 1. Please have your school authority provide predicted results if possible along with an explanation of when your final marks and certificate will be available.

UNIVERSITY OF PENNSYLVANIA		
General admissions information		
Applicants are asked to choose one of the four undergraduate schools to serve as a home base throughout their academic journey. All students gain a strong foundation in the liberal arts and sciences and have the ability to take classes in all four schools. Therefore, we encourage applicants to consistently take classes in the core academic disciplines (English, social studies, mathematics, science and foreign language). We review the school report along with any provided school profile to best understand your high school context, types of courses available, the school's grading scale, and extracurricular or post-secondary opportunities. Students are only expected to challenge themselves academically within the offerings available to them.	**Total undergraduate enrollment**	10k
	Overall acceptance rate	12%
	Global ranking	18
	Average DP score	38
Credit and advanced standing		
The University of Pennsylvania may award credit or advanced course standing to students who have taken IB examinations. Scores warranting credit vary by department. Scores of 6 or 7 in many HL courses will earn credits.		

UNIVERSITY OF SOUTHERN CALIFORNIA		
General admissions information		
The most fundamental expectation entering students at USC is that they will have completed a rigorous high school curriculum in English, mathematics, science, social studies, foreign language and the arts. USC expects that prospective students will take advantage of the highest level of classes offered to them in their secondary school. USC believes that students who undertake an IB curriculum are well-prepared for the rigours of university academic life. IB courses are factored into the admission evaluation process because USC recognizes the extreme rigour of such a curriculum.	**Total undergraduate enrollment**	18k
	Overall acceptance rate	20%
	Global ranking	130
	Average DP score	35
Credit and advanced standing		
Six (6) elective units apiece are earned for scores of five (5) or above on HL exams; or twenty (20) elective units if students earn the IB diploma with a score of 30 or higher. General education credit is available for some history and science exams.		

Ivy League

Ivy League Universities comprise of **eight universities** in the North-Eastern region of US and rank among top fifteen universities in the US.

Pro Tip: Don't just apply to a college because it is Ivy League - there are lots of great universities that are way cheaper (and arguably 'better') than Ivy League

These universities are known for their academic excellence and social elitism. All these universities **consider the performance** of students in IB Diploma Program at the time of admissions. As per the IBO survey, the acceptance rate of IB students by **Ivy universities is up to 18% higher**. Ivy League universities consider IB students as the IB requires a lot of study and discipline.

Pro Tip: If possible, try to interview someone who is at the Ivy League school of your choice (if they did IB, even better!). You can try to find these people by posting on the IBO reddit forum.

You will have to perform well not only in core subjects but in everything. It also requires you to perform activities beyond the class such as community services which helps in your personal growth.

Pro Tip: Since Ivy Leagues are US universities, the IB won't really give you a direct admissions advantage. However, you'll definitely be better prepared for the workload you'll get at a top university.

It should also be kept in mind that every university has different selection criteria. While some of the universities will look for performance in individual courses, some will consider the overall score. Admission requirements are not mentioned clearly on the university websites and thus vary for different institutions. To get a clear understanding of the admission requirement, you can personally get in touch with the university.

It should also be noted that the admission in Ivy league universities starts way before students sit in the IB exam and hence they consider anticipated scores provided by the schools. Also, if the **final IB scores are less than the anticipated score** then the university can withdraw the admission offer.

So, it is always important to provide anticipated scores as accurately as possible. Also, if a school continuously provides inflated anticipated grades then it may affect the school's reputation.

Pro Tip: Ivy League schools tend to focus more on the **extracurricular** (since most who apply have similar excellent grades). You should focus on your essays and extracurriculars

There is **no minimum score** required by the universities as scores are dependent on the course subjects that have been chosen. But to be on the safer side it's always advisable to score more than 38 or at least 6s or 7s in every subject.

Most of these universities would require you to score 7s in HL subjects. For example, if you are planning to do engineering then you probably need to score at least a 7 in Mathematics HL.

Successful candidates usually have a predicted score of 40+ and above to get admission in ivy universities. But remember, Ivy League universities are less particular about the scores rather they consider the holistic performance of the student in IB Diploma program. They also consider your personal background, your abilities, and your leadership qualities. Students should find out the requirement of the university they want to take admission to.

Pro Tip: If you want any chance of getting into an Ivy League, you have to be specialized. For example, you must be REALLY good at something in particular, such as the best debater or track athlete in your state, or a winner of a math Olympiad. (DO NOT DO A MILLION CLUBS as this shows a lack of commitment towards a few things. It shows that you're spread out and aren't really good at anything).

Essay Tips

Here are 10 tips for writing an essay for US colleges:

1. **Before your essay sounds good, it has to sound honest.** Authenticity should always be your starting point. Over the years, I've helped hundreds of students write their personal statements and I can tell you that the most successful essays are always written by the heart before the hand. Why? Because at the end of the day, the value of any personal statement lies in connection, and authenticity is the fabric of genuine connection. It's more than just showing the reader who you are; it's about using your essence to reflect theirs. Think of any film or song that resonates with you. This is precisely the bond that you want to create with your reader. This leads to the next point..

2. **Write for yourself**, not for the school. Of course, you will need to eventually tailor your essay into a mature and professionally sounding piece while following certain guidelines; however, do not make the mistake of writing with the question of "what do colleges want to hear?" I strongly suggest journaling your first draft. In other words, forget the fact that you are writing an admissions essay and simply speak your heart and mind for as if you were writing in a diary or expressing yourself to a friend. This strategy is particularly helpful for students who are struggling to find a meaningful topic. Most importantly, don't be discouraged by a lack of direction; I promise that you will strike gold so long as you keep digging. Expression and discovery always go hand in hand.

3. **It's all in the presentation.** Yes, you should avoid sob stories and cliches; however, this ultimately doesn't boil down to the topic but the context in which you use it.

There is not a single generic topic that is off limits so long as you talk about it in a non-generic way. In other words, it's not just what you say but how you say it. The number of themes available to you are ultimately limited; however, the methods of framing and packaging them are endless.

4. **Do not be dogmatic (or lazy) with your approach.** Often, when I'm working with a student, we touch upon a side-theme in the final draft that paints the essay in a much more impactful and authentic light. When this occurs, I always encourage students to restructure the entire piece to fit that theme, working on the essay three-dimensionally. You may very well find new themes and have new realizations as you are writing. Never be afraid to reconstruct or even demolish your piece if you've found a better foundation to build on.

5. **Write from a place of authority.** After all, it's a personal statement, not a personal plea. You need to have conviction when talking about your life. At certain points, you may ask yourself, "Is this good enough for a college essay?" Replace that question with "If this was the last time I spoke about my life, would this be the story I want to share?" Most of all, don't think that just because you're young, you can't teach the admissions board member something new about life or offer them an interesting perspective.

6. **Not every essay needs to be serious or profound.** You can probably imagine how much drama college admission reads. A little levity will go a long way. If you have a sense of humor, use it! Also, if you are discussing a heavy topic, it may help to find places in your essay for some relief. A mature essay is one that can balance a spectrum of emotions.

7. **Start by showing, not telling.** Ever notice how some television series open with an interesting scene that is not yet explained, followed by the opening credits, then the actual storyline that leads up to it? Try adopting this approach for your essay. Engage your reader from the start with an anecdote. Then format the rest of the essay so that your opening scene starts making sense.

8. **Tie the conclusion back to the introduction.** For instance, if you opened up with an anecdote, refer to it (or something similar) in a new light and with a new understanding in your conclusion. While this strategy is not always necessary, having your essay come full circle is always pleasing for the reader.

9. **Title your essay.** Often underrated, but an interesting title goes a very, very long way and can be the perfect bow for your masterpiece. Sometimes, it's great to think of a title BEFORE you finish your essay; this way, you'll have a better understanding of your essay's meaning as you are writing it. It also helps to look through your essay to see if there are any interesting phrases or words that could be used as a title.

10. **Stick to the theme!** While it may be tempting to veer off into tangents to show how diverse you are, doing so will always dilute the impact of your personal statement. Remember, you don't have a huge word-count to work with. Therefore, your essay needs to be as efficient as possible. Focus on quality, not quantity. Remember, you are not writing a resume; you're creating a story, and the last thing you want to do is to make your reader forget what it's about.

Tips + Advice

The college admission systems in America works a little something like this:

1. ACT or SAT Scores
2. G.P.A (Course rigor such as AP/IB/Honors, and grades)
3. Extracurricular Activities
4. Teacher Recommendations and Application Essays

Literally everything else doesn't really matter in your admissions. If you end up getting poor grades on your IB exams, universities will not care. AP/IB scores are only reported so that students may receive college credits. Most students get accepted to colleges before they even know any of their IB scores/ if they even got the diploma.

Pro Tip: Some of students have suggested that unless you really need to (for other reasons), consider dropping the full Diploma Program and taking IB certificates. A combination of AP, IB HL, and Honor classes to increase your GPA and maintain your workload has worked wonders for some US applicants.

If you go on Reddit to compare yourself to other applicants, you may find yourself deeply discouraged and frustrated. So, we recommend doing this only if you are mentally prepared to see some stellar applicants. Keep your confidence high and remember that your university outcome doesn't define you.

Applying to the US is insanely competitive so just getting a spot is already a big achievement - especially if you are an international student.

Financing

If you pay for university/college in the USA yourself it can be incredibly expensive, but it is possible to receive financial aid. You should make your application for financial aid at the same time as your application. The financial aid is either 'need-based', 'needs-blind' or 'merit-based'.

Although private universities are much more expensive than public universities, do not be discouraged in applying to them, as they are more likely to give students 'grants' (non-repayable) than public universities.

Scholarships can also be applied for separately. There is a scholarship search on collegeboard website.

- First stage is to do a PSAT (Preliminary SAT) here in the school in October of IBY1
- Applicants should register on collegeboard to sign up for SATs and have access to information universities and the application process.
- SATs or ACT are standardized assessment tests. SATs should be sat in May/June of Year 12 and then again in September of IBY2. SAT Subject Tests should be sat in October of IBY2. Registration for SATs should be done two months in advance.
- Many institutions accept 'The Common Application'; others have their own application form.
- 'Early Decision' applications are sent in October/November and regular applications in December, before the January deadlines.

- Part of the application process includes writing an essay from a list of titles on the application form, which can be similar to your personal statement.

At Liberal Arts Colleges students can study a wide range of subjects in the first year before specializing later.

Pro Tip: make absolutely sure that you **RESEARCH** which IB classes you can transfer to your potential college and which you cannot. It would be a shame if you took your first fall semester full of classes you didn't know you would be exempt from!

Course Credit

Many US universities and colleges differ in their approach to offering credit for IB exams. By applying to the US as an IB student, you may be looking to lower the cost of your education or the time it takes to graduate. In addition to finding scholarships, many institutions offer generous course credit for both the full IB diploma and individual DP course exams.

I have known some students that racked up enough college credit during their IBDP that they got to miss up to two semesters of college! Whether or not that is something you actually want is another matter.

While not comprehensive, the IBO provide a long list of colleges to guide you through credit offerings at four-year and two-year institutions:

https://blogs.ibo.org/blog/2018/05/05/getting-ib-credit-at-university/

CHAPTER 9

CANADA

This chapter will provide a brief introduction to the Canadian higher education system and its application process.[21] We will also provide some specific advice for IB students.

Introduction

Throughout Canada's ten provinces and three territories, there are **98 higher education institutions.** Rather than having a centralized federal higher education system, each province and territory has its own distinct education system.

Public and private

There are public and private institutions throughout Canada, however the majority of universities are public institutions. Most public institutions have province-wide admissions requirements, whereas private institutions do not need to follow provincial or territorial admissions requirements. Both public and private

[21] **Adapted from** https://www.ibo.org/contentassets/5895a05412144fe890312bad52b17044/recognition---international-student-guide-ca--march2016---eng.pdf

institutions might offer one or several types of degrees and programs.

Public institutions receive most of their funding from the provincial, territorial and/or federal government, making them generally less expensive to attend than private institutions. Because of the high number of faculty research grants, public institutions tend to have large departments offering a variety of degrees.

Private institutions receive the majority or entirety of their funding from alumni donations, faculty research grants and tuition fees. This makes them more expensive to attend but allows far more resources available to students.

Bachelor's degrees

Bachelor's degrees can be obtained at many higher education institutions and are completed in three or four years of full-time study, depending on the province and whether the program is general or specialized. Some students might complete an honors bachelor's degree, which indicates a higher level of concentration within the subject as well as a higher standard of academic achievement.

Liberal arts education

Liberal arts programs offer courses in the arts, humanities, languages, mathematics, and social and physical sciences, and they aim to cultivate general intellectual capacities. When obtaining a bachelor's degree in the liberal arts, students will specialize in their chosen program (also known as a major or subject) but will also receive generalized education across a spectrum of courses.

Vocational education and community colleges

Canada also has professional, technical, or vocational institutions, as well as community colleges (often referred to as just "colleges"), which tend to provide more specialized courses of study.

Colleges are government-regulated institutions offering various degrees, including pre-professional certificates, two-year associate's degrees and, in some cases, four-year specialized bachelor's degrees. There are more than 150 colleges in Canada, with approximately 900,000 full-time and 1.5 million part-time students. With this option, students can graduate from college and be prepared for a career or transfer to a four-year institution to get a bachelor's degree. Colleges tend to be less expensive than other types of institutions. As college faculty generally do not conduct research, there is a stronger emphasis on teaching, but there are fewer research opportunities for students.

Accreditation

Canada does not have an accreditation system that assesses the quality of higher education institutions, although some provinces have charters or legislation that serves as a substitute. Without a national system, however, you should verify that your degree is recognized in the specific province to which you are applying.

University rankings

There is no official ranking system for higher education institutions in Canada, but there are independent bodies that conduct subjective rankings annually. Canadian universities are commonly ranked among the highest globally. For example, the QS World University Rankings 2014/15 listed five Canadian universities among the top 100 universities in the world.

The Application Process

Who to contact?

There is no centralized application procedure for Canadian institutions; students apply to each institution individually. While some provinces have general admissions requirements for their public institutions, each institution will outline the requirements on its website, alongside any additional requirements for that specific school.

The exception is the province of Ontario, which uses a standardized application system to the public institutions in that province; the Ontario Universities' Application Centre allows students, including international students, to submit one application that is sent to their chosen institutions in Ontario.

Choosing an area of study

While many institutions allow students to study a variety of subjects, most application processes require students to choose a program or area of study that is intended to be their focus throughout their education. Specific programs or faculties within a university might have their own admissions requirements, which may include additional application materials or specific grade or IB score requirements. Because of this, it is important for students to focus on their academic performance and search for institutions that match their interests and level of academic rigor.

The application

There is no national university entrance exam, and each institution has its own admissions standards and evaluation process. Most applications can be completed online, and most institutions require biographical information, education background (including transcripts, IB predicted grades, and IB final grades when available) and intended area of study. Some universities might ask for letters of recommendation, personal essays, or test scores, so students should find out what an application will require well in advance of the application deadline.

Pro Tip: As always, we suggest contacting (by phone or email) your chosen universities and asking any specific questions you may have. They have seen it all and know exactly what you need in terms of permits/tests.

Timeline

It is important to check the application deadline for each institution, as deadlines may vary, but many are in December or January. Some institutions have a rolling admissions process, which means that there might not be a strict application deadline. Decisions from a university might be sent out as early as three weeks after the application is received, or they may take several months. Some institutions offer conditional acceptances, and when final grades and/or IB scores are sent, the offer is either rescinded or made official.

Canadian schools generally accept online applications from **September** onwards, and submission is done directly to the individual institutions (with the exception of schools in Ontario). Students first submit a basic online application, which is a "paid statement of interest", and upload their documents between **February and May**. During this period, students also submit their applications for scholarships/ financial aid. The request for housing will vary between universities, whether it is submitted on initial application or through a separate process. The deadline for students to confirm their offer and apply for immigration documents is around **July**.

Students who have received conditional offers must carefully read the details in their admission letters. If the conditions for admission are not met, the student's admission may be revoked or modified (i.e., it can be modified to probationary status or changed to alternate program).

When it comes to the course selection, students apply for a general area of study (e.g.. Liberal Arts, Education, Engineering) rather than to a specific course. Some schools even allow students to have the first year in university as "undeclared", with the decision made during the students' second year.

Pro Tip: Take note of deadlines and check your emails regularly!

IB Students

Many Canadian higher education institutions offer benefits to IB students. Benefits are determined by each institution individually, but might include credit for certain IB scores, scholarships, or tuition assistance. Some universities allow IB students to enter their institution as second-year students, meaning the undergraduate education will be three years instead of four.

Students taking Diploma Program (DP) courses but not the full diploma might be able to receive credit from institutions for individual courses, but policy is also determined by each institution, and sometimes each individual program or faculty within the institution. Most institutions indicate their IB recognition policy on their website.

There are no special treatments or considerations given to IB students during the initial admissions process. However, if you get in, you do have a chance of getting transfer credits which are granted only to IB, AP and A-Level students when they get above a certain score in some of their subjects. Being an IB student also helps you out because IB gets you used to the rigor of university courses, and to the kind of workload most university students have in their first year.

Pro Tip: While no Canadian university would admit this: our anecdotal evidence suggests that an IB diploma does make you slightly more competitive when applying to schools (who know what the IB is!)

Anticipated grades

It is important to note that the admissions cycle in Canada takes place before IB students even sit exams. Thus, most admissions decisions are based in part on the student's anticipated grades submitted by the school. If a student's final IB scores are significantly below the anticipated grades submitted by the school, it is possible for the university to withdraw its offer. As such, it is vital that teachers and schools report students' anticipated grades as accurately as possible. This is not only important for students' futures, but if a school consistently inflates anticipated grades, it may tarnish that school's reputation with the university

Who Applies to Canada?

In 2014, 3,440 IB students from schools in 115 countries outside of Canada sent 4,832 transcripts to 102 Canadian institutions, an average of 1.4 transcripts per student. This average suggests that more than half of students only send transcripts to a single institution.

Most common source of transcripts coming into Canada

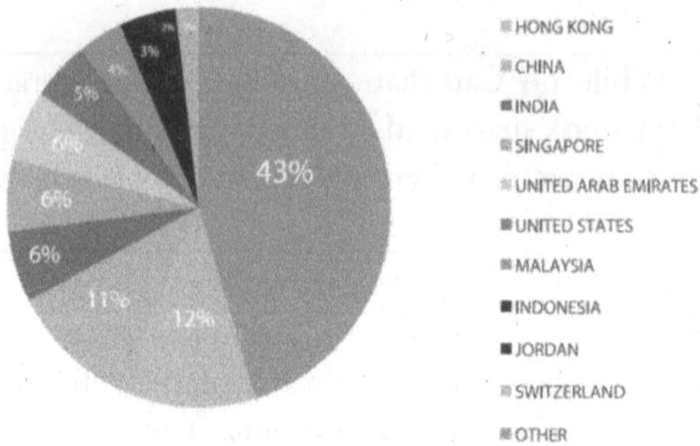

Where do IB Students Apply?

The 10 institutions that received the largest number of IB transcripts in 2014 account for nearly 80% of all transcripts sent to Canada1. All 10 are public institutions, and 9 of the 10 are ranked among the top 500 by QS World University Ranking. Three are ranked in the top 50.

> **Pro Tip:** Make sure to find out how important predicted grades are to your chosen university. Some Canadian universities really don't seem to care, whereas others take a more holistic approach and look at everything together. And there are also those that are very objective and will really focus on your predicted grades. Do your research!

Canadian University Profiles

CARLETON UNIVERSITY

General admissions information[4]

Students pursuing the full IB diploma, three standard level (SL) and three higher level (HL) subjects, are required to have a minimum of 28 points (please note that some programmes are more competitive, so will require higher scores). One subject may have a grade of 3, provided it is offset by a grade of 5 or better in another subject. Prerequisite subjects must have a grade of 4 or better. Specific programmes might have additional course requirements.

Total undergraduate enrollment[1]	22k
Overall acceptance rate[1]	73%
Global ranking[2]	501–550
Average DP score[2]	31

Credit and advanced standing

Students may be awarded advanced standing (transfer) credit for HL subjects with a grade of 5 or better, subject to the discretion of the appropriate faculty to a maximum of 3.0 credits.

Additional considerations

For programmes requiring HL or SL English A, HL English B will also be accepted with a minimum grade of 5.

CONCORDIA UNIVERSITY

General admissions information

Candidates who complete the full IB diploma with a minimum total of 27 points may be considered for admission to the three-year (90 credits) programmes of study (four years of study in the BEng, BA (Early Childhood and Elementary Education), BEd (TESL), BSc in Athletic Therapy, and BFA (Specialization in Art Education)). Minimum scores in prerequisite subjects as well as a higher overall average may be required for competitive programmes.

Total undergraduate enrollment	25k
Overall acceptance rate	71%
Global ranking	411–420
Average DP score	31

Credit and advanced standing

Students who have not completed the full IB Diploma Programme but have IB certificates in individual HL subjects may be eligible for credit.

Additional considerations

The Group 1 English courses (Language A: Literature, Language A: Language and literature, or Literature and performance) (HL or SL) meet English proficiency requirements.

MCGILL UNIVERSITY

General admissions information

DP students must present predicted results of 5 or better in each HL and SL subject as well as school grades during the IB programme that support the predictions. Most programmes will have higher minimum requirements. In addition, students may be required to submit:

- proof of proficiency in English
- placement tests in mathematics and basic sciences
- supporting documentation (that is, official transcripts, external test results, letters of reference or evaluation, extenuating circumstances).

Total undergraduate enrollment	22k
Overall acceptance rate	49%
Global ranking	24
Average DP score	36

Credit and advanced standing

A maximum of 30 credits of advanced standing may be granted for the IB diploma based on HL results of 5 or better.

Additional considerations

Math studies SL is not acceptable for programmes where math is a prerequisite.

QUEEN'S UNIVERSITY

General admissions information

IB diploma candidates must:

- complete the full IB diploma with passes in six subjects with three at HL and a minimum grade total of 28 (excluding bonus points)
- satisfy all admission criteria, including prerequisite courses, for the desired programme
- present a competitive score for the desired programme
- complete and submit a personal statement of experience and supplementary essay.

Total undergraduate enrollment	18k
Overall acceptance rate	42%
Global ranking	206
Average DP score	33

Credit and advanced standing

Students in all faculties and schools may be granted a maximum of 18.0 credit units for HL IB courses completed with a final grade of 5 or higher (6 or higher for some engineering courses).

SIMON FRASER UNIVERSITY		
General admissions information		
Simon Fraser University welcomes IB students from around the world! Our IB students are studying in almost every area at the university, and participating in cooperative education placements all across Canada and in other countries around the world. IB diploma holders with total predicted IB points in the high 20s, including bonus points, will qualify for early conditional admission to most programmes. To be considered for admission, you must meet the English language admission requirement and the quantitative and analytical skills requirement.	**Total undergraduate enrollment**	22k
	Overall acceptance rate	60%
	Global ranking	225
	Average DP score	31
Credit and advanced standing		
Transfer credit is awarded for all SL and HL subjects passed with a grade of 4 or higher.		
Additional considerations		
Completion of DP English A1/A2 or English literature and performance (HL or SL) with a minimum grade of 3 satisfies English language requirements.		

UNIVERSITY OF BRITISH COLUMBIA		
General admissions information		
For standard English language admissions, successful completion of the IB diploma with a minimum score of 24 points, including at least three HL courses, as well as additional points for the core, is required. Additional programme-specific requirements.	**Total undergraduate enrollment**	40k
	Overall acceptance rate	64%
	Global ranking	50
	Average DP score	33
Credit and advanced standing		
All HL and some SL IB courses will be considered for first-year credit.		
Additional considerations		
Where English is the primary language of instruction, English A (SL or HL) is required with a minimum score of 3.		

YORK UNIVERSITY		
General admissions information		
IB diploma with passes in six subjects: three SL courses and three HL courses, OR two SL courses and four HL courses. Minimum IB diploma point scores of 30 or higher recommended (scores of 28 will be considered). Specific programmes might have additional course requirements.	**Total undergraduate enrollment**	42k
	Overall acceptance rate	~80%
	Global ranking	441–450
	Average DP score	31
Credit and advanced standing		
Transfer credit granted for IB courses with HL final grades of 5 or better, depending on the programme (maximum of 30 credits).		

UNIVERSITY OF TORONTO		
General admissions information		
The IB diploma including English HL or SL is accepted for admissions. Prerequisite courses can be presented at either SL or HL. Different areas of study require different predicted scores (more competitive programmes require a higher predicted score).	**Total undergraduate enrollment**	54k
	Overall acceptance rate	69%
	Global ranking	34
	Average DP score	34
Credit and advanced standing		
Credit is granted for HL subjects with a minimum grade of 5.		
Additional considerations		
To demonstrate English language proficiency: The minimum requirement is a score of at least 4 (predicted or final) in HL or SL English A: Literature or English A: Language and literature. English B HL is not acceptable.		

UNIVERSITY OF WATERLOO		
General admissions information		
The University of Waterloo recognizes IB courses as excellent academic preparation for success at the university level. Subjects that are prerequisites for admission to specific programmes should be at HL whenever possible. Where there are more than 3 prerequisite subjects, SL courses will be accepted. For programmes listing HL or SL English A, HL English B with a minimum grade of 5 will be acceptable. For programmes listing HL or SL mathematics, mathematical studies will not be accepted.	**Total undergraduate enrollment**	29k
	Overall acceptance rate	53%
	Global ranking	152
	Average DP score	33
Credit and advanced standing		
The University of Waterloo will consider awarding transfer credits for individual HL IB courses in which normally a minimum final grade of 5 is attained. The maximum number of transfer credits considered varies depending on the programme you're admitted to. Transfer credits will normally be weighted as 1.0 units each (equivalent to 2 courses).		
Additional considerations		
Transfer credit will be considered for the completion of the theory of knowledge and the extended essay with a minimum grade of B (Good) in both. Waterloo equivalent transfer credit is PHIL 1XX (1.0 units).		

UNIVERSITY OF WESTERN ONTARIO–WESTERN UNIVERSITY		
General admissions information		
The minimal requirements for admission of IB candidates are as follows: 1. successful completion of the International Baccalaureate 2. pass in a minimum of six subjects of which at least three must be at HL 3. a grade total of 28 including additional points for the successful completion of the extended essay and theory of knowledge 4. no mark can be less than four.	**Total undergraduate enrollment**	23k
	Overall acceptance rate	31%
	Global ranking	192
	Average DP score	33
Credit and advanced standing		
IB applicants who meet Western's admission criteria are eligible for transfer credit consideration for each HL subject with a score of 5 or higher		

Further Resources:

The Complete University Guide (Canada):

https://www.thecompleteuniversityguide.co.uk/international/north-america/canada/

Top Universities – A guide to studying in Canada:

https://www.topuniversities.com/where-to-study/north-america/canada/guide

Study International:

https://www.studyinternational.com/news/step-step-get-canadian-university-international-student

Applying for a visa:

https://canadianvisa.org/blog/education/how-to-apply-to-canadian-universities

CHAPTER 10

AUSTRALIA

This chapter will provide a brief introduction to the Australian higher education system and its application process.[22] We will also provide some specific advice for IB students.

Introduction

Australia has more than 170 post-secondary education providers, including 43 universities. 39 of these universities are public. Australia's universities are nationally regulated by the Tertiary Education Quality and Standards Agency, which monitors quality and regulates higher education providers using standards from the independent Higher Education Standards Panel. These standards make a concerted effort to cater to international students.

[22] **Adapted from** https://www.ibo.org/contentassets/5895a05412144fe890312bad52b17044/recognition---international-student-guide-aus--march2016---eng.pdf.pdf

International student friendly

Many higher education institutions in Australia are highly ranked internationally and go to great lengths to make the application process smooth for international students. Australian universities have a good deal of autonomy, and each institution determines its own admissions standards. About 25% of students enrolled in higher education in Australia are international students, which is among the highest proportions in the world.

Groups and networks

Many universities in Australia have banded together with similar institutions to form groups or networks.

The Group of Eight (Go8) comprises eight of Australia's leading research universities, and the group has collectively expressed its support for IB students. The Australian Technology Network and the Innovative Research Universities are also prominent university groups.

Although Go8 universities are generally the most highly ranked Australian institutions and are typically associated with the most prestige and highest entry requirements, regional Australian universities with lower entrance requirements also have many outstanding students and strong teaching and research.

Degree types

Students can pursue one of three degrees after completing the IB Diploma Program: an Associate Degree, a Bachelor Degree or a Bachelor Degree (Honors). An Associate Degree takes two years to complete and is career-focused. Students can get an Associate Degree to better prepare them for their career, to receive a certificate in their field and/or as a step towards getting a Bachelor Degree.

A **Bachelor Degree** usually takes four years to complete and is more in depth than an Associate Degree. It prepares students for their careers, as well as for postgraduate study. Bachelor Degrees in professional fields can sometimes take more time. Some students choose to do a double or combined program, which results in earning two Bachelor Degrees. Some institutions offer "graduate-entry Bachelor Degrees", which cannot be entered directly from senior secondary school and typically are in professional specializations.

In some professional specializations, Bachelor Degrees using Honors terminology (for example, Bachelor of Engineering with Honors) may be awarded on the basis of academic achievement. In such cases, an increased course load and/or short thesis may be required.

Bachelor Degree (Honors) programs include a coherent and advanced development of knowledge and skills in one or more specializations in addition to research principles and methods. A significant research thesis or project is required.

The Application Process

There are three ways to apply to Australian higher education institutions.

Direct application: Students from outside of Australia can apply directly to an institution, following that institution's application procedures. In this case, students must fill out separate applications for each course and institution to which they are applying.

Education agents: Students can also apply through a licensed Australian education agent. There are various agents in Australia, and each institution might be partnered with one or several of these agents. Institutions typically list which agent(s) they partner with on their websites. Agents help students put together their applications and supporting documents and send the application materials to the institution(s). Students might choose to work with agents if they need help with the admissions process, obtaining student visas or preparing to study in Australia. IDP Education is one of the largest agent organizations and is co-owned by 38 Australian universities.

Tertiary Admissions Centers: Finally, there are offices called Tertiary Admissions Centers (TAC) that process applications to a number of institutions within a particular state or group of states. These TACs cover Queensland, South Australia/Northern Territory, Western Australia, New South Wales/Australian Capital Territory and Victoria. Check the individual TAC sites to see which institutions they cover. TACs provide students with relevant application information, as well as facilitate the application and offer processes. Some institutions might not accept a TAC's international application process, so international students should check whether the course they are interested in encourages direct application from international students.

Choosing an area of study

To study at an Australian university students typically apply to specific courses within a university. A course is a particular area of study, such as psychology or biology, and most classes a student takes will be related to this course. Thus, it is important that applicants are clear about what they would like to study at the time of their university application.

Some universities do allow students to apply to the university itself or to a broader degree within the university (for example, Bachelor of Arts or Bachelor of Commerce) that encompasses several course options. Students should be sure to understand the particular admissions processes at institutions to which they are applying.

The Australian Tertiary Admissions Rank

The Australian Tertiary Admissions Rank (ATAR) shows Australian students' achievement in relation to other students. The ATAR is calculated from students' academic results prior to applying to universities, and in order to receive an ATAR students must complete the necessary courses in Australia.

International students do not receive an ATAR. Most Australian higher education institutions accept IB results as an equivalent to an Australian Year 12 qualification, and there may be a scale in place to convert scores to ATAR.

Testing

There are several tests that certain courses and universities might require of applicants. For example, the International Students Admissions Test (ISAT) is required for international applications to some medicine, dental or veterinary courses and is offered in centers around the world.

The Special Tertiary Admissions Test (STAT) is a general test that assesses a variety of subjects and competencies, but it is generally used by students who don't have a recent Year 12 qualification.

English language proficiency testing is also quite common for students from non-English speaking backgrounds and may even be a requirement to obtain a student visa from the Australian government.

Other tests may be required for certain courses, so it is important that students are aware of the requirements of the courses and institutions to which they'd like to apply well in advance.

Receiving and accepting offers

After applying, students might receive offers from the university directly or through a TAC, depending on how they applied.

Offers can be unconditional, meaning the student has been accepted to study at the institution. Conditional offers are contingent upon the student fulfilling certain conditions, such as a minimum number of points for IB diploma results and a minimum score on specific IB subjects. A university might choose to decline an application rather than giving an offer.

Once final IB results have been sent to the institution and the requirements of conditional offers are met, students must respond to the offers and pay the required fees by the set deadline. At this point, students are officially enrolled in a course and on track to begin study at the institution. There are several deadlines and fees throughout this process, so it is important for students to be aware of dates and communications with the institution or TAC.

Timeline

Many Australian higher education institutions operate on a two-semester basis, with the first semester being February through June, and the second being July through November. Application deadlines might vary from institution to institution, but to start in February, deadlines are generally sometime in October.

IB Students

The IB diploma is recognized by all major tertiary institutions in Australia. Some universities offer advanced placement, credit, and bonus schemes for Diploma Program (DP) students.

Most Australian higher education institutions accept IB diploma results as an equivalent to an Australian Year 12 qualification, and students' IB results will be used as a ranking system instead of an ATAR. In some cases, higher education institutions have a conversion scale in place to convert IB scores to ATAR. More information about the IB and Australian rankings can be found on the UAC website, which includes a conversion scale of IB results to UAC rankings.

Anticipated, predicted and final IB scores

Due to the application timeline, offers may be made based on anticipated IB scores submitted directly by the student's school to the university or by predicted IB scores the student's school submits to the IB and the IB in turn reports to the university. To confirm an offer, final IB results may need to be submitted either to the TAC or directly to the institution.

Who applies to Australia?

In 2014, 1,355 students from IB World Schools in 89 countries sent 3,046 transcripts to 65 Australian institutions, including the TACs, an average of 2.25 transcripts per student. A total of 1,075 transcripts were sent to TACs, leaving 1,971 (nearly two-thirds) sent directly to the institutions.

Most common source of transcripts coming into Australia

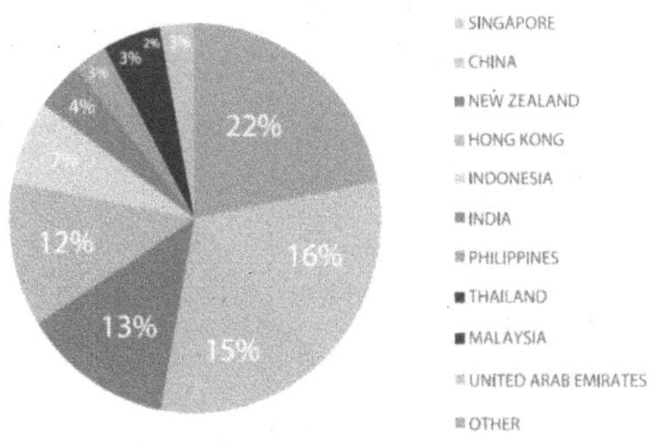

Where do IB students Apply?

While the TACs are among the single largest recipients of transcripts (as they typically represent several institutions), nearly two-thirds of transcripts from IB students outside of Australia bypass the TACs and are sent directly to the institutions.

Over 85% of these transcripts were sent to just 10 universities. All 10 are ranked in the top 300 universities by the QS World University Ranking, and 5 of them are ranked in the top 50. All 10 are public institutions, and all of the Go8 universities are represented.

Australian University Profiles

AUSTRALIAN NATIONAL UNIVERSITY		
General admissions information[3]		
Australian National University (ANU) accepts the IB diploma and bi-lingual diploma as equivalent to an Australian Year 12 qualification. If you are an international student completing a high school or university qualification outside Australia, you need to submit your application directly to ANU. If you are applying from an IB programme in Australia, you need to apply through UAC.	**Total undergraduate enrollment**[4]	8k
	Overall acceptance rate[5]	83%
	Global ranking[6]	19
	Average DP score[7]	34
Example course requirements[8]		
Business Administration BA: 30 points overall		
Additional considerations		
Presentation of an IB diploma where the language of instruction is English satisfies the university's English language requirements.		

MACQUARIE UNIVERSITY		
General admissions information		
Macquarie University knows that as an IB student, you are distinctive. You have a "switched on" approach to learning and you're actively engaged with the world around you. At Macquarie you will be nurtured as a global leader of tomorrow through unique programmes like PACE (Professional and Community Engagement), and the Global Leadership Program. If you're studying in Australia but have your eye on bigger things, you'll also be a perfect fit for our Global Leadership Entry Program, giving you access to exclusive on-campus learning activities while you're still in high school.	**Total undergraduate enrollment**	22k
	Overall acceptance rate	81%
	Global ranking	229
	Average DP score	29
Example course requirements		
Commerce BA: 29 points overall		
Additional considerations		
IB students in Australia who excel in subjects relating to Macquarie's programmes can receive Academic Advantage Bonus Points to increase their entry score. Macquarie University accepts English A Literature or English A Language and Literature at Standard or higher level; English B at Higher Level with a Grade of 4 or more; English B at Standard Level with a Grade of 5 or more.		

MONASH UNIVERSITY

General admissions information

Entry requirements are specific to each course. Typically it is required for the full diploma to be awarded.

Total undergraduate enrollment	40k
Overall acceptance rate	82%
Global ranking	67
Average DP score	32

Example course requirements

Business BA: 28 points overall; at least 4 in English standard level (SL), 3 in English higher level (HL), 5 in English B SL or 4 in English B HL, and at least 4 in mathematics SL/mathematical studies SL or 3 in mathematics HL/further mathematics

Additional considerations

IB English A or B may fulfill English language requirements, but requirements are specific to each course.

ROYAL MELBOURNE INSTITUTE OF TECHNOLOGY (RMIT)

General admissions information

Completion of the IB diploma, including English, with a minimum score of 25 to 31 depending on the programme of study. Some programmes may have additional prerequisites.

Total undergraduate enrollment	23k
Overall acceptance rate	99%
Global ranking	273
Average DP score	30

Example course requirements

Bachelor of Business (International Business): 25 points overall

Additional considerations

English language requirements are fulfilled by a minimum of 4 in English A HL or SL, 4 in English B HL or 5 in English B SL.

UNIVERSITY OF QUEENSLAND

General admissions information

The University of Queensland welcomes IB students from around the world. We recognize that the IB diploma is a comprehensive and challenging programme. Our experience is that IB diploma graduates are incredibly well prepared for university success. The programme's international flavour, academic rigour and emphasis on inquiry-based learning means that IB students enter university with a global outlook, an excellent work ethic and the critical thinking skills to ensure they achieve great results. IB students may be offered credit or exemption for selected courses. Depending on the degree programme, students may be awarded up to one semester (8 units) credit.

Total undergraduate enrollment	35k
Overall acceptance rate	80%
Global ranking	46
Average DP score	32

Example course requirements

Business Management BA: 29 points overall and IB English and any IB mathematics course

Additional considerations

The following fulfill English language requirements:
A grade of 4 or better in Language A: Literature or Language A: Language and Literature (previously English A1 and English A2) at HL or SL.
A grade of 5 or better in Language B (previously English B) at HL or SL.
Note – Literature and Performance is not accepted.

UNIVERSITY OF SYDNEY

General admissions information

Each course lists a minimum IB score required to obtain entry to that course. Typically it is required for the full diploma to be awarded.

Total undergraduate enrollment	28k
Overall acceptance rate	98%
Global ranking	45
Average DP score	34

Example course requirements

Economics BA: 31 points overall

Additional considerations

Completing the Diploma Programme in English satisfies English proficiency requirements.

UNIVERSITY OF ADELAIDE		
General admissions information		
Completion of the IB diploma, plus any programme-specific requirements is sufficient for entry.	**Total undergraduate enrollment**	16k
	Overall acceptance rate	100%
	Global ranking	113
	Average DP score	31
Example course requirements		
Economics BA: 25 points overall		

UNIVERSITY OF MELBOURNE		
General admissions information		
The University of Melbourne guarantees admission to a course when an IB student achieves the required score as listed on the course website, has met the prerequisites, and has satisfied the English language requirements.	**Total undergraduate enrollment**	22k
	Overall acceptance rate	57%
	Global ranking	42
	Average DP score	35
Example course requirements		
Commerce BA: Guaranteed entry with an IB total score of 35 points, grade 4 in mathematics SL/HL or further mathematics		
Additional considerations		
4 or higher on IB English HL or SL satisfies English language requirements.		

UNSW AUSTRALIA		
General admissions information		
Though there are no specific prerequisites for undergraduate degrees, candidates must study certain subject areas in their last year of high school. Specific courses list IB scores that will gain students direct entry into that course.	**Total undergraduate enrollment**	28k
	Overall acceptance rate	90%
	Global ranking	46
	Average DP score	34
Example course requirements		
Commerce BA: 34 points overall		
Additional considerations		
The following fulfill English language requirements: 4 or above in English A: language and literature HL/SL, English A: literature HL/SL, or English B HL.		

Further Resources:

Study International step-by-step guide:

https://www.studyinternational.com/news/step-step-get-australian-university-international-student/

Australian government's guide to applying to study in Australia:

https://www.studyinaustralia.gov.au/english/apply-to-study

CHAPTER 11

NETHERLANDS

This chapter will provide a brief introduction to the Dutch higher education system and its application process.[23] We will also provide some specific advice for IB students.

Introduction

The Netherlands is one of the most developed nations in the world, known for its tolerant and liberal ethos. It has a high quality and international system of higher education that dates back to the 16th century. Despite its relatively small size, the Netherlands has 13 universities ranked in the top 300 and 5 within the top 100. In addition to a wide range of courses in Dutch, the Netherlands has more than 2,100 international study programs and courses taught in English. You can view available options at www.studyinholland.nl. These factors, combined with relatively modest tuition fees, make the Netherlands one of Europe's most popular destinations for higher education.

---

[23] **Adapted from** https://www.ibo.org/contentassets/5895a05412144fe890312bad52b17044/recognition-international-student-guide-nl-nov-16-en.pdf

Pro Tip: Holland is becoming an ever increasingly popular option amongst IB students - so make sure to consider it! Feedback from my students has been excellent, and it's not too expensive.

Quality assurance

NVAO guarantees the higher education system's standard level of quality and alignment with the Qualifications Framework for the European Higher Education Area. All degree programs offered by research universities and universities of applied sciences are evaluated according to established criteria. All accredited programs are listed in the Central Register of Higher Education Study Programs (CROHO).

Types of HEIs

There are three types of higher education institutions (HEIs): government-funded, government-approved, and private. There are two main types of institutions: research universities and universities of applied sciences. Thirteen of the research universities, the Open University and more than 50 universities of applied sciences are considered government-funded.

Research universities mainly offer research-oriented programs in an academic setting. However, many of their programs are in a professional setting or have a professional component and most graduates go on to careers that are not necessarily research related. There are 14 research universities in the Netherlands, including the Open University, but collaboration with universities of applied sciences is common. University colleges, which are generally part of a research university, also offer undergraduate programs, mainly in liberal arts. The research universities vary in size, with enrolments ranging from 6,000 to 30,000 students.

Universities of applied sciences (*hogescholen* in Dutch) generally offer professional programs that focus on the practical application of the arts and sciences to prepare students for a specific career.

Practical work experience and internships are often an important part of the professional study programs offered at these institutions. The largest universities of applied sciences enroll 20,000 to 40,000 students.

Institutes for international education are a third, smaller branch of higher education with programs designed specifically for international students. These institutions typically only offer non-degree programs or courses leading to a Master's degree.

Degree types

The basic types of degrees offered in the Netherlands include Associates, Bachelor's, Master's and Doctoral. Both research universities and universities of applied sciences offer bachelor's or master's degrees. You first obtain a bachelor's degree (first cycle), you can then continue to study for a master's degree (second cycle) and then a doctoral degree program (third cycle).

Associate degrees, offered only at universities of applied sciences, are typically 2-year professional programs leading to a career or continued study in a bachelor's program. Currently, around 60 associate degree programs are available in a variety of fields.

Bachelor's degrees are offered at both research universities and universities of applied sciences. There is quite a wide range of programs in a variety of disciplines offered in the Netherlands.

Universities of applied sciences offer degrees in a wide variety of disciplines and formats, including honors programs, majors and minors, and dual programs. Most are four-year degrees structured around an introductory year (*propedeuse*), followed by the main phase of three years. These degrees focus on the skills and competencies needed for a job in a specific field, and thus often offer practical experience through internships, classroom instruction, projects, and group assignments.

Research universities offer both discipline-based bachelor's degrees and interdisciplinary liberal arts degrees at university colleges. These programs teach the academic and scientific skills associated with a traditional academic discipline and are meant to prepare students for further study as well as employment. The content of the programs can vary from broad to very specialized, but generally include a course in research methodology and a bachelor's thesis.

Type of institution	Degrees and duration
Universities of applied sciences	Associate (Ad): 2 years
	Bachelor (B+field of study/BSc/BA): 4 years
	Master (M+field of study/ MSc/MA): 1-2 years
Research universities	Bachelor of Science/Arts (BSc/BA): 3 years
	Master of Science/Arts (MSc/MA): 1-2 years
Institutes for international education	Master of Science/Arts

Applying to Dutch HEIs

In most instances, students apply directly to the study program within the institution they are interested in. Programs within a single institution may have significantly different entry requirements. In some cases, they may even have completely separate application procedures.

Entry requirements

Typically, for entry into a Dutch bachelor's degree program a Dutch *vwo* diploma (research universities) or *havo* diploma or *mbo* diploma, level 4 (universities of applied sciences) is required. Of course, numerous other international qualifications, including the IB diploma and in some cases the IB CP certificate, are accepted.

Admission requirements for most study programs are now expressed in terms of specific tracks that students need to have completed in their secondary school program. The four specific tracks are known as "subject clusters". They are culture and society, economics and society, science and health or science and technology. These changes have affected the admission requirements for students with foreign and international qualifications, including the IB diploma. However, for many English-taught programs these profiles are not necessary.

Pro Tip: We highly suggest checking out EIB entrance requirements matrix[24] - which provides a very convenient way to compare Dutch universities and courses as an IBDP student.

At times, additional other criteria must be met. Because of the limited number of available places for some courses, candidates may be selected by an admissions committee. Therefore, meeting minimum entry requirements does not guarantee a place in the program. Academic performance, international experience, motivation, and other factors may all be taken into account.

For access to certain programs, particularly those in the fine arts, students must demonstrate the required artistic abilities. The only

[24] https://drive.google.com/file/d/13XCaC3QeZGbg7HSr1BaqpLLzrOjyhyit/view

access requirement for the Open University is that applicants be at least 18 years of age.

As undergraduate programs in the Netherlands are mostly in Dutch or English, students will need to demonstrate a sufficient level of fluency in the relevant language.

As with any European Union nation, the visa process differs according to citizenship. **EU nationals** do not need a visa to study in the Netherlands. **Non-EU nationals**, depending on nationality, may need to apply for a provisional residence permit, known as an MVV (*Machtiging* tot *Voorlopig Verblijf*). The website *Study in Holland* has the relevant information.[25]

The quota (numerus-fixus) system

Certain oversubscribed courses, primarily in the medical sciences, are deemed "*numerus fixus*". Until 2017, to get a place in one of these courses, students need to be successful in a weighted lottery. Per academic year, students are allowed to apply for a maximum of two study programs with a decentralized selection procedure. These two applications can also be for the same study program at two different institutions. For Medicine, Dentistry, Physiotherapy and Dental Hygiene, students may only choose one.

As of 2017/18, the Dutch government has abolished the lottery system, and allowed HEIs to select the students for their own *fixus* programs. This is called a decentralized selection procedure. In this decentralized procedure, a committee assesses the application based on criteria such as motivation, personality, and previous academic performance. The criteria may differ between institutions and programs.

[25] www.studyinholland.nl

Application process

There are two systems for applying to Dutch universities: directly to the institution and through Studielink. The path depends on the university course to which you are applying. Studielink is used as an online application system for some courses, but all applicants must register by law in Studielink regardless of the application process, otherwise their application will not be finalized. Students who are applying for a *numerus fixus* program must register in Studielink before 15 January. It is best to check with the website of the specific course you intend to apply to for the most accurate information on application procedures.

Typically, students who apply via Studielink will then hear from their university of choice on whether they satisfy the requirements. The exact course of the procedure depends on the type of program. If a student is considered "admissible", they can begin working with the university directly on fulfilling any additional entry requirements. Programs with open admission require "matching", and programs with decentralized selection have their own placing procedures. If students satisfy all of the requirements they can be admitted and enroll.

Cost

Tuition fees vary depending on whether the student is from the EU, or whether they are attending a public or private institution. The average annual fee for EU students is €1,950. Non-EU students should expect to pay between €6,000 and €15,000. However, there are various scholarship options available. The fees at private institutions can be substantially higher. Some institutions have application fees as well.

Timeline

For most programs, Studielink opens in October prior to the starting year, and applications are typically due between January and May. Note that for *numerus fixus* programs, you must complete the application in Studielink by 15 January. After students register and/or apply in Studielink, the university informs students on any further application procedures. Between May and September, the university may assist students with finalizing program selection. The basic steps of applying through Studielink are:

1. Register in Studielink

2. Complete application via the intended university/program website

3. Upload the application documents

4. The University assesses admissibility

5. Follow the admissions procedure

6. Complete registration and pay tuition fees

IB Students

As a Dutch national policy, IB diploma holders are admissible to higher education in the Netherlands. As the admission cycle generally takes place before IB results are released, DP candidates may be provisionally admitted on the basis of their anticipated score reported by their schools. However, students must always be able to verify their results and that they obtained the full IB diploma after results are released.

There are some minimum course requirements for entry into Dutch programs.

o Economics, econometrics and (international) business studies:

o Mathematics SL

o Universities of applied sciences:

o Mathematics HL

o Physics HL (chemistry at HL instead of physics for certain fields)

o Chemistry at SL (or physics at SL when chemistry is offered at HL)

o Medical and related fields:

o Biology at HL

o Chemistry at SL (including options for organic and higher physical chemistry)

o Physics at SL (including options for biomedical physics and optics)

o Mathematics SL

Please note that universities in the Netherlands are autonomous and admission requirements may vary with institution.

Pupils who successfully complete the IB Career-related Program are eligible for higher professional education (HBO) in the Netherlands. To compare the IB subjects with the Dutch subject clusters, EP-Nuffic has carried out a deficiency study; see the EP-Nuffic website for the study results (only in Dutch).

Since no full diploma has been obtained, DP Courses are not sufficient for admission to higher education in the Netherlands, neither higher professional education (HBO) nor academic education (WO). Students who offer individual DP courses in combination with a national diploma or qualification may be considered on a case-by-case basis.

Exemption from the Dutch language test can be granted if a candidate has taken Dutch as language A (SL or HL) or as language B at HL.

Who Applies to the Netherlands?

In 2015, 1,407 IB students from schools in 104 countries requested to send 2,084 transcripts to 57 Dutch institutions: an average of 1.5 transcripts per student. This makes the Netherlands the 5th most popular destination for international IB transcripts, and the 7th most popular destination overall. Given recent trends, it is conceivable that the Netherlands will become the 4th most popular destination for international IB students within the next few years.

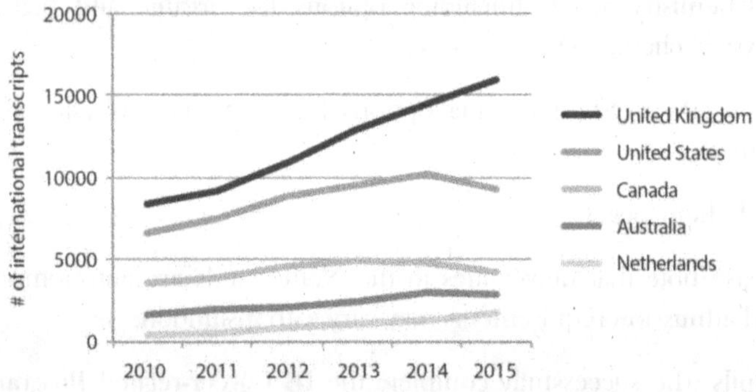

The make-up of IB students sending transcripts to the Netherlands is incredibly diverse. Domestic transcripts only account for 18% of the total, and those from Dutch passport holders abroad only account for another 17%. Thus, 65% of all IB students sending transcripts to the Netherlands are international students who completed the DP outside of the Netherlands. Additionally, they come from very diverse locations, though mostly from the EU and Asia.

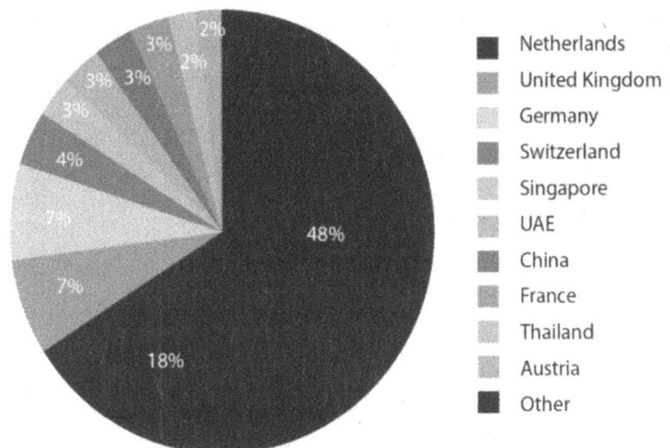

Figure 2: Origins of IB transcripts sent to the Netherlands in 2015.

Where do IB Students Apply?

After aggregating individual programs and university colleges under parent institutions, 57 HEIs received transcripts from IB students, and 9 of these received more than 50% of transcripts. More than half of these were ranked in the top 100 global research universities, and all but one were ranked in the top 300.

IB specific information on each of these universities is outlined below.

Dutch University Profiles

DELFT UNIVERSITY OF TECHNOLOGY		
General admissions information		
If you hold an IB diploma and have passed the specified IB examination subjects, you are eligible for admission to the Bachelor programmes of TU Delft.	Total undergraduate enrolment	11k
	Global ranking	64
	Average DP score	33.6
Example course requirements		
Aerospace Engineering (English stream)	English + mathematics HL + physics HL	
Applied Earth Sciences (English stream)	English + mathematics HL + physics HL	
Note: TU Delft has decided to require mathematics HL, effective as of intake 2018. For the transition year of intake 2016–2017 + 2017–2018, students with a mathematics SL will still be considered for admission.		
Additional considerations		
If your IB schooling has been in the English language, you are exempted from the English language requirement. Holders of an IB-diploma with the subject "Dutch B" and wishing to study in a Dutch-medium programme, must take an assessment at TU Delft, and may be required to enrol in part of the Dutch language course. If your IB diploma includes neither Dutch A nor B, you may be required to take the entire Dutch language course.		

ERASMUS UNIVERSITY ROTTERDAM		
General admissions information		
The IB diploma is accepted as an entry qualification. Entry requirements and prerequisites vary by undergraduate programme.	Total undergraduate enrolment	13k
	Global ranking	126
	Average DP score	33.6
Example course requirements		
BSc International Business Administration: • minimum of 33 points (TOK, EE and CAS included) • minimum grade of 5 for mathematics SL **OR** minimum grade of 4 for mathematics HL • minimum grade of 5 for English A SL **OR** minimum grade of 4 for English A HL **OR** minimum grade of 5 for English B HL		
Additional considerations		
You need a good command of the English language before you can apply for a degree programme at Erasmus University. Exemption from English proficiency exams is possible for scores in English A HL or SL or English B HL.		

LEIDEN UNIVERSITY

General admissions information

The IB diploma awarded after the completion of the full IB Diploma Programme, is sufficient for general admission. IB certificates are only taken into consideration in combination with national diplomas that grant admission to higher education. When you apply, kindly include official predicted grades from your school and ensure that the levels of all subjects, including language subjects, are clearly stated (HL, SL, A or B, and so on).

Total undergraduate enrolment	14k
Global ranking	95
Average DP score	32.4

Example course requirements

BA Liberal Arts and Sciences: Global Challenges: Students must present an IB Diploma taught in English with a minimum score of 4 in mathematics SL or HL or a minimum of 5 in mathematical studies. Students may be exempted from the remedial maths course if they present an IB Diploma taught in English with a minimum score of 4 in mathematics SL or HL or a minimum of 5 in mathematical studies.

Additional considerations

You can be exempted from English proficiency requirement if you have an English-taught IB diploma. An IB diploma with Dutch A SL or HL or Dutch B HL may qualify for exemption from the Dutch language requirements.

THE HAGUE UNIVERSITY OF APPLIED SCIENCES

General admissions information

The International Baccalaureate diploma is an acceptable qualification for our three-year programmes. THUAS offers a wide range of international Bachelor programmes in English, several of which offer an accelerated track for advanced students (including IB graduates).

Total undergraduate enrolment	25k
Global ranking	N/A
Average DP score	30.1

Example course requirements

No programme specific entry requirements could be found.

Additional considerations

If you obtained an IB diploma, you might qualify for an exception to the English proficiency requirements. Please contact the Enrolment Centre and ask for details.

UNIVERSITY OF MAASTRICHT

General admissions information

The IB diploma is accepted as an entry qualification. For some programmes, there are additional subject requirements and/or language requirements.

Total undergraduate enrolment	10k
Global ranking	169
Average DP score	32.7

Example course requirements

BSc International business: Mathematics SL or HL or further mathematics is required

UTRECHT UNIVERSITY

General admissions information

The IB diploma is accepted as an entry qualification. For some programmes, there are additional subject requirements and/or language requirements.

Total undergraduate enrolment	20k
Global ranking	94
Average DP score	33.7

Example course requirements

BSc Pharmaceutical Sciences: Achieve the IB diploma with chemistry HL, physics SL and mathematics SL. Mathematical studies is not accepted.

Additional considerations

The IB diploma taught in English satisfies the university's language requirements.

TILBURG UNIVERSITY

General admissions information

To be admitted to a Bachelor's programme at Tilburg University, you will need to meet several application requirements: diploma requirements, English language proficiency requirements, and for some of our programmes also mathematics requirements. The IB diploma is an acceptable qualification for entry. A passing score in mathematics SL is required for Business and Economics courses.	Total undergraduate enrolment	5k
	Global ranking	293
	Average DP score	31.3

Example course requirements

BA/BSc in Liberal Arts and Sciences: Students must earn the IB diploma with English as one exam subject.

Additional considerations

You meet the English language requirements if you have obtained an IB, including English language as a part of the curriculum.

UNIVERSITY OF AMSTERDAM

General admissions information

International Baccalaureate: Diploma or official record from the IB Office in Geneva >24 points and mathematics at SL or HL (mathematical studies is not accepted).	Total undergraduate enrolment	17k
	Global ranking	55
	Average DP score	33.2

Example course requirements

No IB specific programme requirements could be found. However, some programmes may have prerequisite course requirements. Students are advised to check with the individual faculty they are interested in for further details.

Additional considerations

Applicants with an IB diploma may be exempt from the English proficiency testing requirements.

UNIVERSITY OF GRONINGEN

General admissions information

The IB diploma is accepted as a qualification for admissions into undergraduate programmes.	Total undergraduate enrolment	18k
	Global ranking	100
	Average DP score	32.9

Example course requirements

BSc International Business: Mathematics SL or HL is required.

Final Tips

Consider this key advice given by EIB admissions on applying to Dutch Universities:[26]

Firstly, make a decision on which types of university you would like to apply to. You are free to apply to all of the types mentioned above, but please remember that research universities tend to be more academically rigorous, focus on critical thinking and independent study (essentially, the "why"). Applied science universities are normally more focused on building skills needed for employment and have a greater emphasis on collaborative work (essentially, the "how"). If you want to study liberal arts, it is likely that you will apply to a university college, and we encourage you to check the admissions criteria for these colleges as they will differ from their research or applied science namesakes.

Secondly, please bear in mind the application process and availability of certain subject choices. You can put down up to four choices. Of these, two can be Numerus Fixus courses whilst one can be medicine, both of which could have subject requirements. Therefore, please look at the relevant university webpages to confirm the course requirements and application process for your chosen course. It is also likely that you will require a CV and motivational letter for competitive courses and could be invited to an admissions day.

Linking to this, please do not be fooled by the low offer that Dutch universities often give out. These may be attractive to British students applying to UK universities as well, but the first year will be as thorough if not more so at a Dutch university.

Finally, please take the opportunity to go and see the university during an open day or even as part of your admissions day. This will enable you to see the university first-hand and talk to both

---

[26] https://www.eibadmissions.com/resources/a-guide-to-applying-to-dutch-universities/

lecturers and students about their daily lives. We wholeheartedly encourage you to gather as much information and experience as possible before applying, as this will help you make the right decision. Additionally, being in-person at an admissions day, rather than conducting an interview via Skype, will help you make a strong first impression.

CHAPTER 12

GERMANY

This chapter will provide a brief introduction to the German higher education system and its application process.[27] We will also provide some specific advice for IB students.

Introduction

Germany offers a robust and renowned higher education system, and many individual institutions have established strong names within particular fields. The country offers a high quality of life, support and scholarship opportunities and good employment prospects. Germany's public universities offer the majority of courses free of charge, for both domestic and international students, and most major German cities have at least one highly ranked research university.

Institution and degree types

---

[27] Adapted from https://www.ibo.org/contentassets/5895a05412144fe890312bad52b17044/recognition-international-student-guide-germany-2019-en.pdf

Germany has around 400 higher education institutions; more than 100 universities; over 200 Universities of Applied Sciences (UASs; *Fachhochschulen*); and almost 100 specialized institutions such as medical universities, art schools and colleges of public administration. UASs focus on practical, applied and professionally oriented education, offer courses that lead to bachelor's or master's degrees, and are known for close relationships with businesses, internships, work placements and practical projects.

The bachelor's degree is the most common undergraduate degree. A bachelors will usually take six semesters (three years) to complete and can focus on one main subject (a single honors degree, or "mono bachelor") or a combination of several subjects(a joint honors degree or combined bachelor's).

Some courses offer a *Diplom* or *Staatsexamen. Diplom* courses tend to be offered in the technical and engineering fields, while the Staatsexamen can be taken in medicine, dentistry, veterinary medicine, pharmacy, law, food chemistry, and some teaching degrees.

Pro Tip: Germany, like Holland, is becoming ever more popular amongst IB students who normally would have gone to the UK. You can get a high-quality education without spending thousands.

Requirements for Admission

Undergraduate admissions procedures and requirements in Germany are somewhat complex and can vary considerably depending on the field of study, state, institution, and even individual department. If you think you'd like to pursue higher education in Germany, you are strongly encouraged to consider well in advance what you want to study and where.

For most areas of study, the individual universities are responsible for the final admissions decisions, but some fields have national level admissions procedures. There- fore, you should determine in advance whether you want to go into a field with national admissions or not, and you should inquire at the university of your choice about all the necessary prerequisites.

There are a few important points you should understand before beginning the application process in Germany.

The Hochschulzugangsberechtigung

In general, to study in Germany you need to have a recognized *Hochschulzugangsberechtigung* (HZB) or "higher education entrance qualification". For German students, this is typically the Abitur, but the HZB may come in many forms, including the IB diploma.

If you don't meet the minimum qualifications then you must take a preparatory course at a Studienkolleg and then a compulsory assessment test known as a *Feststellungsprüfung*, covering areas relevant to the intended course of study. After successfully completing the assessment, graduates are permitted to study the corresponding subject areas anywhere in Germany.

Statements of comparability

Students with German nationality who do not have a German Abitur may need to obtain a "Statement of Comparability" (*Bescheinigung*) to study at a public university. These are official documents issued by the central education office in the same state as the university. International students need to apply directly at the university.

Not all states have such recognition centers, so be sure to check with your intended university well in advance.

Numerus Clausus

Some degree courses (i.e., dentistry, medicine, veterinary medicine, and pharmacy) have more applicants than available seats. Such courses are referred to as *Numerus Clausus* (NC), Latin meaning “limited” or “closed”, and applicants need to compete for admission to these courses. Some courses have national restrictions applying to all German universities, and others may have a local restriction specific to the state or university.

The actual minimum NC requirements change every semester based on current supply and demand and are calculated based on the grades of the received applications. So, when applying, the exact level of the NC may be unknown, but the cut-offs from previous semesters are good indicators. Certain subjects may be weighted more heavily than others (i.e., mathematics and physics for an engineering course).

Admission types

Once admitted, entitlement is either **direct** or **indirect** and either **general** or **subject-specific**. Direct enrollment is possible for all courses without admission restrictions (i.e., non-NC).

- Direct: the applicant can start their degree straight away.

- Indirect: before beginning their degree, the applicant must pass the *Feststellungsprüfung*.

- General: the applicant may study any subject.

- Subject-specific: the applicant may only study subjects in a specific field.

Uni-assist

Uni-assist is a centralized admissions portal, run by the German Academic Exchange Service (DAAD), and handles international applications for its member universities.

An online application via uni-assist's online portal may be compulsory, although a separate application direct to the university may also be required. Some national NC courses are also processed through uni-assist.

The Application Process

Unless applying for a national NC course, Diploma Programme (DP) students will typically apply directly to the individual university in which they are interested. Applications from IB students are generally handled in the same fashion regardless of where the student took the DP.

Admissions processes vary between institutions and between courses within institutions. Some universities may require applications to go through www.uni-assist.de, while others may have their own application forms. Sometimes both online and print applications are required and both must reach the university by the application deadline. Make sure you check the information from your chosen university before applying.

Students applying to public universities may need the relevant state board of education to provide a Statement of Comparability during the application process, so ensure that you know the location of the university, the state's requirements, and factor this extra step into your timeline.

Applying to NC courses

DP students (assuming all conditions are met) are usually considered to have the same status as German citizens with regard to admissions and compete with German applicants for the majority of NC course seats. All others compete for the remaining places (usually 5–10%). As mentioned, medicine, dentistry, veterinary medicine, or pharmacy have restricted admission at all public universities, and the application and admission procedures for these NC courses are run by the *Stiftung für Hochschul- zulassung*.

For other courses, DP applicants may apply directly to the universities or via uni-assist. Students who are required to pass the *Studienkolleg* or are applying for a preparatory pre-study German course, typically need to apply through uni-assist.

Some tips for applying to NC courses

- Send applications to a variety of universities/courses
- Choose less popular locations
- Understand the point system and how to compile additional points
- Apply for summer semester admission, which may have fewer applicants

Application documents

Apart from the average required grade, universities may also define additional criteria, such as letters of motivation, tests, or selection interviews. To ensure the best chances of acceptance, take care to provide all the documentation requested, make sure all your documentation is certified, and ensure that you've filled out all your information correctly. An application fee may be charged. While specific documents and processes will vary, you'll typically be asked to submit:

- an officially certified copy of the HZB with the sub- jects and grades from the final two years of high school in the original language
- a certified translation of the subjects and marks
- proof of language proficiency (an officially certified copy or online verification code)

Language requirements

The language of instruction is German in most courses, requiring international applicants to submit proof of proficiency in the German language through a language test result or by taking a preparatory course.

Under certain circumstances, DP Language A German and Language B German higher level (HL) courses may satisfy language requirements. If not, you may need to take a university-approved test. You should contact the university to determine their eligibility for entry.

For NC courses

For applications to NC courses, the average grade for an IB diploma will be calculated in the state in which the certification is evaluated. The calculation of the average grade (N) will be based on the total points (P) and on a maximum of 42 points (Pmax) and a minimum of 24 points (Pmin). Any extra points achieved will also be taken into consideration. Points totals between 42 and 45 will be equated to the German average grade of 1.0. The calculation is made using the following formula:

$$N = 1 + 3\,\frac{P_{max} - P}{P_{max} - P_{min}}$$

N = *gesuchte Note (Durchschnittsnote)*

P = *im Zeugnis ausgewiesene Gesamtpunktzahl*

Pmax = 42 *Punkte (IB-Gesamtpunktzahl ohne*

Zusatzpunkte) Pmin = 24 *Punkte* (*unterer Eckwert*)

N = 1.0 (*für* $42 < P < 45$)

$$N = 1 + 3\,\frac{P_{max} - P}{P_{max} - P_{min}}$$

N = *gesuchte Note* (*Durchschnittsnote*)

P = *im Zeugnis ausgewiesene Gesamtpunktzahl*

Pmax = 42 *Punkte (IB-Gesamtpunktzahl ohne*

Zusatzpunkte) Pmin = 24 *Punkte* (*unterer Eckwert*)

N = 1.0 (*für* $42 < P < 45$)

Verifying results with uni-assist

If you wish to apply before DP results are issued, uni-assist can verify your exam results online until the end of August in the same year. In this case, you must approach your school in May and give permission for the IB to supply your exam results to uni-assist. Students must notify uni-assist that the IB has made their results available. There is no automatic procedure to verify all available test results from the IB. Please make sure you submit the following documents:

- Your IB diploma with an official Transcript of Grades issued by the IB

- Your certificates from your final two years in the IB Program sent in authenticated form from your school–regardless of whether your exam results have been verified online or not

- Your certificate from Year 10 or certification proving at least 12 consecutive school years

- An Approval of Qualifications document from Germany if you have one (not compulsory)

The *Gemischtsprachige* IB Diploma

The IB-Agreement also includes the *Gemischtsprachige* IB Diploma (GIB), a bilingual IB diploma that includes three subjects taught and assessed in German: history, biology, or chemistry and either language A or language B. Students also have the option to take theory of knowledge (TOK) and mathematics: analysis and approaches in German. Applicants have to meet the same requirements as stated above concerning subjects and course level and marks/grading.

Where do IB Students Apply?

In 2015, 1,660 transcripts were sent to Germany by 579 students from 74 countries. That's 2.9 transcripts per student. Just over a third of transcripts came from students undertaking the DP in Germany, and the remainder came from a wide variety of origins including Europe, Latin America, and Asia. Of the 1,071 transcripts sent from outside of Germany, about half came from German passport holders.

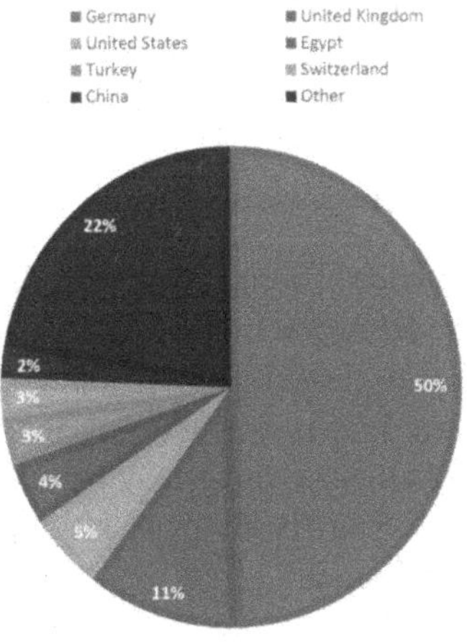

Germany has some fantastic universities, but the lack of instruction in English is a sticking point preventing it being a real alternative for most international school students. With the exception of Universities like Jacobs, which despite offering a very high service level, is also charged at equivalent rates to the UK, there are not many courses offered in English (yet!). With rising interest from overseas, and growth of the IB and other similar programs within the German school system, it will not be surprising to see more and more courses being offered either in English, or via blended approach. The free education is certainly an attractive proposition, and many German universities are very widely recognized, but unlike other countries, you really need to put the hours in to establish quality and ensure the institutions you are applying to understand your home qualification and levels of both English & German.

Where IB students send transcripts

IB students send transcripts to a wide variety of institutions in Germany. Over 200 in fact. The most common transcript destinations are unsurprisingly uni-assist and the state education boards, because uni-assist processes applications for a number of institutions, and the state boards require the transcripts for verification purposes. However, around 60% of transcripts went directly to the higher education institutions.

Due to the varied nature of admissions procedures in Germany, it is impossible for the IB to determine exactly which universities DP students are applying to. Listed below in alphabetical order are the 10 bodies that received the most transcripts in 2015. Four of these are universities. Nonetheless, there may be other universities that take in greater numbers of IB students via admissions procedures other than direct application (i.e., NC courses).

INSTITUTION	DESCRIPTION
Bezirksregierung Düsseldorf	State board for Dusseldorf. Universities in the state include: University of Dusseldorf and UAS Dusseldorf, among others.
Hochschulstart.de	Central body that processes applications for over 700 local NC courses and medical related national NC courses (i.e. medicine, veterinary medi- cine, dentistry and pharmacy).
Jacobs University	Jacobs University is a private, independent university in Bremen offering courses in English. Undergraduate applications are accepted through the Common Application. A score of 6 or 7 in IB English A: Literature, and English A: Language and Literature is accepted as proof of English proficiency.
Niedersächsisches Kultusministerium	State board for Lower Saxony. Universities in the state include: Leibniz University of Hanover, University of Gottingen, Osnabruck UAS, Lune-burg University and University of Oldenburg.
Rheinisch-Westfälische Technische Hochschule Aachen	RWTH Aachen University is a research university in Aachen, North Rhine-Westphalia. IB students require a federal recognition of their university entrance qualification certificate issued by the Certificate Recognition Office in the respective federal state to apply.
Ruprecht-Karls-Universität Heidelberg	Heidelberg University is a public research university in Heidelberg, Baden-Württemberg. The application procedure is determined by the course you wish to apply for, but applicants must apply to the univer-sity for all subjects. Proof of German proficiency may be required.
Technische Universität München	The Technical University of Munich is a research university with campuses in Munich, Garching and Freising-Weihen-stephan. For IB specific application information, see: http://www.tum.de/en/studies/application-and-acceptance/applicants-with-an-ib-international-baccalaureate-diploma/.
Uni-Assist	Central application processing body for member institutions and some national NC courses.
Zeugnisanerkennungsstelle Für Den Freistaat Bayern	State board for the Free State of Bavaria. Universities in the state include: Technical University of Munich, Ludwig Maximillian Univer-sity of Munich, University of Erlangen-Nuremberg and the University of Wurzburg.
Zeugnisanerkennungsstelle Regierungspraesidium Stuttgart	State board for Baden-Württemberg. Universities in the state include: Karlsruhe Institute of Technology, University of Tubingen and Heidel-berg University.

CHAPTER 13

HONG KONG

This chapter will provide a brief introduction to the Hong Kong higher education system and its application process.[28] We will also provide some specific advice for IB students.

Introduction

One of the world's most competitive cities, the Hong Kong Special Administrative Region (HKSAR) is home to some of Asia's, and indeed the world's, finest universities. It is also ranked in the top 10 cities for international students. Education in Hong Kong is largely modelled on the UK system, but undergraduate programs are typically a mix of British and American systems.

Education is overseen by the Education Bureau (EDB), who report to the government of Hong Kong rather than the Chinese Ministry of Education.

[28] **Adapted from** https://www.ibo.org/contentassets/5895a05412144fe890312bad52b17044/recognition-international-student-guide-hk-en.pdf

Prior to the 1960s, higher education in Hong Kong was mainly for the elite, with very few students admitted to only a single university. Through the 1980s and into the new millennium, education underwent significant expansion and development. In 2012, undergraduate programs at public universities moved from a three-year specialized focus system, similar to that of the UK, to a four-year holistic, student-oriented approach more aligned with the US model. Recently, the government of Hong Kong also introduced additional benefits to international students: the quota for non-local students at publicly funded institutions increased to 20%, scholarships for international students were strengthened (up to HK$80,000), and visa and employment restrictions were relaxed.

Academic culture

While the education system may be more Western in organization, academic attitudes are heavily influenced by traditional Chinese culture. There is a strong value placed on examinations, hard work and meritocracy.

Students are encouraged to understand the larger process of learning, to manage and supplement their academic progress independently, and to develop practical skills by focusing on the "real-world" application of what is taught.

Along with the change to the four-year model, Hong Kong universities have enhanced interdisciplinary studies, service learning and exchange programs to put a greater emphasis on whole-person development, global citizenship, and international outlook.

Institution types

There are about 20 degree-granting higher education institutions in Hong Kong, which offer a wide array of programs. Eight of these institutions are publicly funded universities. In addition, about another 20 institutions offer a variety of locally accredited sub-degree programs. Courses, programs, entry requirements and fees vary considerably, and students are strongly advised to confirm details directly with the intended institution.

Higher education institutions in Hong Kong include the following:

• Publicly funded universities: The eight public universities funded by the University Grants Committee (UGC) each offer associates, bachelors, masters, and doctoral degrees, and some provide sub-degree programs. Most programs are taught in English.

• Vocational Training Council (VTC) institutions: Member institutions offer vocational and undergraduate technical programs focusing on applied skills in general fields such as arts and sciences.

• Self-financing programs: Eleven self-financing institutions provide both sub-degree and degree level programs. The government has recently been developing this sector, including a HK$3.5 billion education fund for scholarships and quality enhancement efforts.

• Specialized institutions: There are a number of public and independent institutions that offer specialized instruction areas, such as the publicly funded Hong Kong Academy for Performing Arts.

• Non-local courses: There are some 1,100 courses offered by foreign providers in Hong Kong.

Degree types

There are multiple post-secondary study pathways available in the region, including sub-degree programs, associates, bachelor's, and graduate degrees. Many of these tracks have multiple entry and exit points. Upon completion of secondary school, students can enroll directly on an undergraduate degree course or pursue another degree type that may allow them to move into an undergraduate program later.

Undergraduate degrees

Bachelor's degrees are now typically four years in length for full-time students. Each university offers a range of study programs across general study areas divided into faculties, each with a unique set of major, minor, credit and entry requirements. This model allows students to complete general studies and nominate one or more "major", or specialization, within their study area. In addition to their major(s), students usually select a "minor"–a secondary specialization with less credit requirements than the major. Double-degree programs are also possible at some institutions. Course load options can be somewhat flexible, allowing students to take more or less courses in a given semester (within limits) as long as they meet the overall requirements by the end of the program.

Associate and other degrees

Students who do not wish to pursue an undergraduate degree, or do not gain entry to a bachelor's degree program, may pursue an associate degree or a higher diploma. These courses often articulate with a degree course later on. It is also sometimes possible to gain a course transfer from a successfully completed higher diploma or associate degree into an overseas degree program with some credit transfer.

The Application Process

Hong Kong's reputation as a competitive city certainly holds true for its university admissions. The number of places available for undergraduate degrees is substantially less than the number of students who meet the entry requirements for general admission. So, qualifying for a program may not necessarily lead to admittance. At a minimum, applicants are generally expected to have completed a secondary education program and gained satisfactory results.

Local students with the Hong Kong Diploma of Secondary Education (HKDSE) results apply to all publicly funded universities through the Joint University Programs Admission System (JUPAS). However, local IB students and international students apply through the Non-JUPAS/International Admissions Schemes directly to a university through its website.

Course selection

It is very important that you research each separate subject you might study in detail. Although most universities have general admissions requirements, there may be faculty-specific requirements as well.

Admissions

Specific entrance requirements vary across institutions, study level and subject area. However, broadly speaking, applicants are primarily considered based on the nature of their academic background and academic achievements. Many faculties will include an admissions interview as part of the process. Most universities will require proof of proficiency in English language, as most programs are taught in English. Some may also have additional language requirements.

It is important for applicants to convey understanding of, and enthusiasm for, their field of study while outlining relevant academic achievements and skills. However, international applicants should be aware of the local cultural attitudes towards boasting or self-promotion.

Timeline

The Hong Kong academic year begins in September and runs until April or May. Students are advised to begin researching prospective institutions a year prior to their start date. Dates and deadlines vary between institutions, but applications are usually accepted from

September to April for the following academic year. In most cases you should be prepared to apply by the end of December. Some universities also have mid-year intake rounds.

Fees

While tuition fees for local students are relatively modest, fees for international students can be higher. Fees vary between programs, but international students can expect to pay between HK$100,000–HK$150,000 per year in undergraduate tuition. Some universities may charge additional fees.

The Hong Kong government does provide scholarships to outstanding local and international students, and financial assistance to qualified local students in need.

Information for IB students

Despite its competitive environment, Hong Kong is generally very favorable towards IB students. The IB diploma is recognized by all publicly funded universities and most self-financing institutions. They understand the qualification well, and most institutions have specific IB policies outlined on their websites.

Both local and non-local IB students should apply directly to the individual institution(s) they are interested in attending.

In general, Diploma Program (DP) candidates will need to have been awarded the IB diploma as meeting the minimum entry requirement. Owing to the competition for university places in Hong Kong, a total score above 30 points will likely be required to gain entry into an undergraduate degree program at one of these institutions. In some cases, the bar may be set much higher.

Many institutions grant advanced standing to higher-performing IB students. The exact number of transfer credits are determined by the individual university faculties after the candidate has been admitted.

Who applies to Hong Kong?

Despite its relatively small size and the cap on the number of university places for international students, Hong Kong is among the most popular higher education destinations in the world for IB students.

In 2015, 22 Hong Kong institutions received 3,195 transcripts from 1,558 students (just over two transcripts per student). About 35% of those undertook the DP in 50 different countries outside of Hong Kong.

Interestingly, the UK is the only country outside of Asia sending significant numbers of students to Hong Kong, but 90% of those UK students held Chinese or Hong Kong passports. This suggests that while it is a major international destination, Hong Kong may offer a decidedly "pan-Asian" experience.

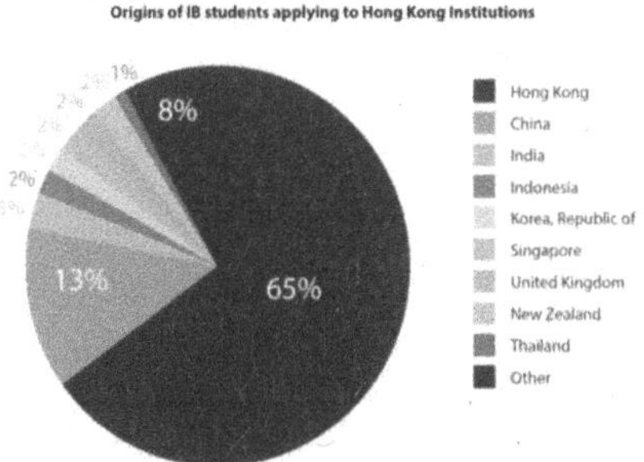

Where do IB Students Apply?

In 2015, 22 Hong Kong institutions received transcripts from IB students. The bulk of these went to the region's publicly funded universities. Six universities received more than 50% transcripts last year. Of these, four were ranked in the top 100 research universities in the world by QS, and in 2015 all of them were ranked in the top 300.

Hong Kong University Profiles

HONG KONG BAPTIST UNIVERSITY		
General admissions information		
The university adopts a policy of broad-based admissions for most of its programmes, where students can enhance their overall understanding of their desired discipline in the first year, and can then make the best choice of major. **IB diploma** holders are eligible to apply for admission to undergraduate degree programmes. IB applicants should request the IB to send scores to the university electronically.	Total undergraduate enrollment Global ranking Average DP score	7k 278 32.4
Example course requirements		
No faculty-specific prerequisites could be identified.		
Additional considerations		
Scholarship opportunities are available to outstanding local and overseas **IB diploma** holders. No separate application is required. The university will identify outstanding candidates for the award of scholarships upon successful admission. **Advanced standing**: IB applicants once admitted may apply for transfer of units up to 15 units if they have taken equivalent courses in other institutions previously. A grade of 4 or above in any group 1 course or English B HL, or 5 or above in English B SL meets the university's English language requirements.		

THE CHINESE UNIVERSITY OF HONG KONG		
General admissions information		
General admissions requirements include receiving the IB diploma, a grade 4 or above in English language and Chinese language. There may be exemptions for the Chinese language requirement at the discretion of the Faculty Dean concerned. Additional faculty-specific requirements may apply.	**Total undergraduate enrollment**	15k
	Global ranking	44
	Average DP score	36.8
Example course requirements		
BSc Science: Two of the following subjects taken at HL: chemistry, biology, economics, geography, mathematics, further mathematics, physics.		
Additional considerations		
Applicants who meet specific requirements may apply for "Admission with Advanced Standing". The minimum number of units for graduation for students admitted with Advanced Standing may be reduced by up to 24 (normative period of study may be reduced by up to one year). Additionally, candidates who have completed only the first year of IB Diploma studies with outstanding results may be considered for admission under special circumstances on individual merit case-by-case.		

CITY UNIVERSITY OF HONG KONG		
General admissions information		
Award of an International Baccalaureate (IB) Diploma is necessary for admission to first-year studies. For Advanced Standing I, a minimum diploma score of 30 (out of 45) is required.	**Total undergraduate enrollment**	13k
	Global ranking	55
	Average DP score	33.1
Example course requirements		
No faculty-specific prerequisites could be identified.		
Additional considerations		
IB applicants may apply for admission to first-year studies in a degree programme or admission to a major with Advanced Standing I (non-senior-year). Students admitted with Advanced Standing I (non-senior-year) must achieve a minimum requirement of 90 credit units for graduation, subject to the requirements of individual colleges/schools/academic units.		

THE UNIVERSITY OF HONG KONG		
General admissions information		
HKU particularly values the IB Diploma as the learning pedagogy in programme mirrors that of HKU. An IB diploma with 30 points out of 45 is the minimum entry requirement, but competitive scores will depend on the degree programme. For example, for Medicine, Dentistry or Law, scores would have to be in excess of 40 out of 45. On the other hand, scores of 32 to 35 would be the usual minimum for programmes with large quotas. Actual scores for successful applicants will also be dependent on the number and quality of applications received that year.	**Total undergraduate enrollment**	13k
	Global ranking	27
	Average DP score	37.1
Example course requirements		
BSc Science: Students must take at least one of the following subjects: biology, chemistry, mathematics, physics.		
Additional considerations		
A grade of 4 or higher in any group 1 course or English B HL, or a grade of 5 or higher in English B SL fulfill the university's English language requirements. Students must also earn a grade 4 or above in a language other than English. IB applicants with at least seven years of secondary education at the time of admittance will be granted 30 credits of Advanced Standing. An extra 6 credits will be granted to applicants who fulfill the exemption criteria for Core University English. Advanced Standing will be granted automatically and separate application is not required. Note: Award of Advanced Standing may differ by faculty.		

THE HONG KONG POLYTECHNIC UNIVERSITY		
General admissions information		
The general admissions requirements are a minimum score of 24 with at least grade 4 in two HL subjects and at least a grade 4 in English.	**Total undergraduate enrollment**	16k
	Global ranking	111
	Average DP score	32.3
Example course requirements		
No faculty-specific prerequisites could be identified.		
Additional considerations		
IB students may be given credit transfer upon admission to the four-year full-time undergraduate degree programmes. Normally, they will be given credit transfer from 9 credits to a maximum of 25% of the award requirements, depending on their previous study and grade attainments. Normally, there is no need for new students to apply for entry credit transfer, and the number of credits required will be shown on the offer notice. Students who have not been given credit transfer at the admission stage may submit an application after enrollment, together with relevant supporting documents.		

THE HONG KONG UNIVERSITY OF SCIENCE AND TECHNOLOGY		
General admissions information		
As a university with a global outlook and international ambience, HKUST welcomes applicants from any corner of the globe. IB students should submit their applications directly to the university via the online application system. HKUST is committed in supporting outstanding students who choose to pursue their higher education with the university. Receiving the **IB diploma** is a minimum qualification for entry, but the mid-50% score range for the 2015 intake was 36–40 (including bonus points).	**Total undergraduate enrollment**	9k
	Global ranking	36
	Average DP score	37.1
Example course requirements		
BSc Science: One HL subject from physics, chemistry, biology, mathematics.		
Additional considerations		
The **"University Admission Scholarship Scheme for IB Diploma Holders"** will be awarded to top students based on academic merit without separate application. Students with IB Total Points (including Bonus Points) 36 or above will be awarded with scholarships ranging from HK$10,000 (36-37) to full tuition plus living allowance (45). IB Diploma candidates/holders are automatically considered for the awards based on their verified IB Total Points. IB students admitted in 2014 on average received 21 advanced credits on entry. These students have more flexibility in pursuing their interests and, should they decide to do so, can graduate in less than four years. A grade of 4 or higher in any group 1 course or English B HL, or a grade of 5 or higher in English B SL fulfill the university's English language requirements.		

Lightning Source UK Ltd.
Milton Keynes UK
UKHW040711250522
403498UK00001B/53

9 781916 345140